ARGOOD OIL AND GAS CORPORATION

402 Hales Building

Phone 7-5771

OKLAHOMA CITY, OKLA.

AN INSTITUTION DEVOTED TO THE PROFITABLE DEVELOPMENT OF OIL

OWNERS & OPERATORS OF
KEENE-OKLA OHIO NO. 1
CATALINA NO. 1
CATALINA NO. 2
IN OKLAHOMA CITY GUSHER FIELD

USED 1/7/37

April-24-34 MAN-DRINKS UP

Mr Ripley
Dear Sir
I am sending you a Picture of my self of drinking up-not down on a step ladder I did the act 26 yrs ago in Denver Colo on a Bet of 25.00 that I could drink a Bottle of Soda or Beer without drop going down my throat as you see in the Picture. it going up.
you can have the answer in the paper the next day if you wish
I concured the Idea of two mules drinking water from a Brook of 45% Grade down a steep Bank; after they drank 4 or 5 swollo they would throw there heads to one side or the other, + kept on repeating untill there thirst was satisfied. I was 16 yrs old at the

PAGE 144

CABLE ADDRESS: SLITEL

Sligh and Tyrrell
INCORPORATED

MUSIC • ENTERTAINMENT • STAGE UNITS
140 NORTH DEARBORN STREET • CHICAGO • PHONE STATE 2850

Feb. 1, 1938.

Mr. Bob Ripley,
% W M A Q,
Chicago, Ill.

Dear Bob:

BELIEVE IT OR NOT ---

JACKIE DEL RIO, not only chews his steak, but he chews the table as well! Not only his own table, but the next table and all the chairs! Yes, TWO TABLES AND SIX CHAIRS all in one mouthful! The enclosed photograph is no fake.

To prove it, Jackie will appear on your radio program - and do his stuff in full view of your studio audience, and to the delight of your millions of listeners - many of whom have been so hungry at some time or other, that they could "eat the table" themselves!

If this intrigues your interest, as it does ours, we will gladly arrange the details immediately. As an added attraction, Jackie, who is only "five feet in height" weighing 115 pounds, and young, will actually pick you up in his teeth and carry you around the microphone seated in your chair!

Yours very truly,
Fred Joyce
FRED JOYCE, PRESS AGENT
SLIGH & TYRRELL, INC.

FJ/L

NEW YORK • CLEVELAND • DETROIT • LOS ANGELES

PAGE 39

E. M. COULTER, PRESIDENT — ESTABLISHED 1886 — M. A. SMYTHE, VICE PRES. AND SEC.

ROANOKE National Business College

NATIONAL BUSINESS COLLEGE BUILDING

BUSINESS MEN FURNISHED BOOK KEEPERS AND STENOGRAPHERS — GRADUATES ASSISTED TO POSITIONS

USED 2/5/3

ROANOKE, VIRGINIA
March 30, 1936

FILE No.

NAMES

Mr. Robert L. Ripley,
c/o King's Syndicate,
235 East 45th Street,
New York City.

My dear Mr. Ripley:

Enclosed is a photograph which we believe will be of interest to you.

The small man on the right is E. E. East of West Virginia. The larger man on the left is E. E. West of east Virginia. These two men met recently at the National Business College in Roanoke, Virginia. Mr. East is a student this year at this school, and Mr. West was a student in former years and is now Assistant Cashier of the First National Exchange Bank of Roanoke.

Each of these gentlemen has given me permission to pass this information along to you.

Sincerely yours,
M. C. Townsend
Personnel Director

MCT:ER
Enc.

The Emblem of the Efficient School

PAGE 178

ROBERT FERN DALLAS TEXAS MAR 1933

CAN BALANCE A QUARTER ON ITS EDGE ON HIS NOSE

BY BEARING DOWN COIN HARD - HE MAKES CREASE ON NOSE -

WHILE MAKING CREASE - HE SHAKES HEAD IN "YES" MOTION - RELEASING COIN OCCASSIONALLY TO SEE IF COIN WILL STAND ALONE -

WHEN COIN STANDS ALONE - HE RELEASES FINGERS - THEN SLIGHTLY, BUT QUICKLY SHAKES HEAD IN "NO" MOTION -

SIMPLE TO WATCH IT -- IT'S NOTHING MORE THAN MOMENTUM -

TAKES HIM ABOUT 3 MINUTES TO GET CONTROLL OF COIN -

CAN HOLD IT FOR ONLY APPROXIMATELY 25 SECONDS -

I HAD TO USE A BLACK BACK GROUND TO SHOW COIN - HAVE SPOILED SEVERALS PICTURES - HAVING HAD DIFFICULTY IN SHOWING COIN AGAINST OTHER THAN BLACK BACK GROUND -

FERN IS LEAVING FOR SAN ANTONIO MAR. 13 - IF EXCEPTED - DESIGNATE DALLAS - (HE ASKS)

Robert Fern

W. L. MONTGOMERY
116 E 104 ST
CHICAGO

PAGE 49

Dear Mr. Ripley

A Compendium of Curioddities from the Believe It or Not! Archives

Dear Mr. Ripley

A Compendium of Curiodditities from the Believe It or Not! Archives

Compiled and edited by
Mark Sloan, Roger Manley, and Michelle Van Parys

A META Museum Project

Second Edition

Library of Congress Cataloging-in-Publication Data
Dear Mr. Ripley : a compendium of curioddities from the Believe It or Not! archives / compiled and edited by Mark Sloan, Roger Manley, and Michelle Van Parys. –1st ed.
p. cm.
ISBN 1-893951-05-7
1. Curiosities and wonders. I.Sloan, Mark. II. Manley, Roger.
III. Van Parys, Michelle. IV. Ripley, Robert LeRoy, 1893–1949.
V. Title: Dear Mister Ripley.
AG243.D47 2002
031.02–dc20 92-23246

Book design by Eric Baker Design Associates Inc, NY
Cover airbrushed by Ron Bertuzzi, NY

Printed in the United States of America

This book is dedicated to the memory of

ROBERT LEROY RIPLEY

1890–1949

R.I.P.

Contents

Note to the Reader. All of the photographs in this book came from the immense Believe It or Not! Archives. This is the backup documentation that Ripley required for his cartoons. Each caption is followed by the date that the cartoon appeared. Some of the photographs have visible pencil marks on them, which were likely applied by Ripley himself as he used the original photographs as the basis for his cartoon drawings. **None of the photographs in this book is the result of trick photography.** There are occasional examples of hand-applied modifications, but these additions are obvious.

The authors and publisher disclaim any responsibility for injuries that may result from readers emulating any of the activities depicted in this book.

If you know of an unbelievable fact or unusual item you think should be in our next book, please contact:

Archive Department
Ripley Entertainment Inc.,
5728 Major Blvd., Suite 700
Orlando, Florida, 32819
or
email: publishing@ripleys.com

Albert J. Smith of Dedham, Massachusetts, was billed as The Busiest Man in the World: A One-Armed Paper Hanger with Hives.

Ripley
Believe it or not!

Preface: Prospectors of the Peculiar

When we met in the middle after starting from both ends of the 300-foot-long files of the Ripley's Believe It or Not! Archives, we may have felt like driving a golden spike or cracking a champagne bottle, but instead stumbled to a trio of massage therapists to get the kinks worked out of our backs. The arduous task of tunneling through the millions of letters and drawings and photographs sent in to Robert Ripley over the decades of his worklife—ourselves hunched over, straining our eyes in narrow passageways between the ranks of file shelves, sifting through the Strata of the Strange (as we affectionately called it)—might faintly compare with working a mine, but the sense of discovery, the excitement we felt each time we pulled some new nugget of weirdness from the already enriched ore, sustained us through the whole long job. We had entered a realm of outlandish frontiers and alternate realities that had been discovered in otherwise ordinary neighborhoods and farms scattered across the continent. We were miners working the Mother Lode of Oddity; we had become prospectors roaming through the territory of the unusual.

Dr. A. Boinker of Jersey City, New Jersey, demonstrates his unusual specialty of being able to jump from a train going 20 miles per hour—backwards! (June 23, 1932)

Our first encounter with the Ripley Archives occurred in 1988, while we were working on a book called *Hoaxes, Humbugs, and Spectacles: Astonishing Photographs of Smelt Wrestlers, Human Projectiles, Giant Hailstones, Contortionists, Elephant Impersonators, and Much, Much More!* Under the aegis of the META Museum (a conceptual, unincorporated creative collaboration founded by the authors in 1985), we had visited nearly a hundred state and local historical societies, archives, and photographic collections throughout the United States and Canada, hunting for visual records of "human spectacle." At our first eyeball-to-emulsion encounter with only a few of the many hundreds of thousands of never-before-published images in the holdings of Ripley's Believe It or Not! we knew right away we had another book to do, this time concentrating only on this one great collection.

The enormity of the task nearly overwhelmed us at first. Robert Ripley, and later his staff, had filed correspondence relating to the cartoon chronologically week by week for more than half a century. We decided to narrow our focus by concentrating primarily on the three decades of Ripley's worklife, and even that left more than sixteen hundred weeks of correspondence to sort through, most of it handwritten on everything from banana leaves to aluminum foil. It would have been a huge undertaking to read mail received by any well-known person over a thirty-year period, but this was Ripley, who received more mail than anyone in history, and the job seemed nearly impossible.

After the first few achingly long days we were dismayed with our progress: we had proceeded toward each other only a matter of inches, and it looked as if we would grow old before we even came within sight of each other working from opposite ends of Ripley's career. But as our skills at sorting slowly developed, the speed picked up. For instance, if while flipping through a file our eyes fell on the words scrawled in pencil across the top of a sheet of foolscap

"Dear Mr. Ripley, I'm the eleventh . . ."

we'd learned to flip immediately to the next letter, because the writer is about to say, "I'm the eleventh son of the eleventh son born at eleven o'clock on November 11, 1911," like scores of others who excitedly contemplated their own numerological uniqueness and wrote Robert Ripley to say almost exactly the same thing. A *little* fascinating, maybe, if mainly for the way they kept turning up in the files, but these finds weren't particularly visual, and photographic imagery was our quarry. We could also skip any letter that didn't include a photo, although most did.

The next file might open to a yellowed snapshot of a man gingerly presenting a shaving brush with only a few bristles still attached to the handle, and again we'd come to know it was safe to keep flipping: this is the ninth or tenth time this day we'd run across a shaving brush that miraculously served its owner for decades, finally entering the realm of almost unbelievable longevity—or not, as we'd quickly decide, and go on ahead.

The Marshall Brothers Dry Creek Holstein Ranch in Cheboygan, Michigan, produced a bull (through artificial breeding) that displayed an upside-down map of the lower peninsula of Michigan on its side! (December 11, 1953)

Often the letters sent in to Ripley would include poignant descriptions of the sender's financial plight, along with instructions detailing how much money was to be sent, under the mistaken impression that Ripley or his newspaper syndicate paid huge rewards for each entry. Belief in this rumor, so widely held it nearly constituted a folk legend, was undoubtedly fueled by the highly publicized Ripley contests in which amazing prizes (cars, airplanes, etc.) actually were given away. Most senders were content to receive the customary *Ripley's Believe It or Not!* book for their efforts. A great many people sent in their suggestions hoping to become famous, and indeed anyone who actually appeared in the cartoon *was* famous across the nation, albeit briefly. This was such a momentous occasion to many that they left word it should be mentioned in their obituaries!

After tickling through file after endless file, we began to suspect that oddity, like the universe itself, might be finite. Only Ripley's Believe It or Not! had amassed enough raw data on oddity to make such a conclusion possible.

This isn't to say we became jaded. Quite the opposite: we saw so much weirdness, so many odd things in such a compressed time, that the commonplace now seemed the exception. We'd wonder, Why is it that when we crack an egg to make breakfast, there's only one yolk inside? We'd come to feel shortchanged with any egg in the Ripley Archives that had only two yolks.

So many armless guitar players turned up in the files that we began to marvel at anyone who strummed an instrument with mere hands. "What's wrong with that guy?" we'd find ourselves asking. "Why isn't he at least playing it upside down or underwater?"

No, when we say oddity is finite—and this is a realization come to after looking at millions upon millions of the oddest things in the world—we mean that a taxonomy presented itself, and a pattern something like a Peri-ODD-ic Table began to emerge. The ordinary world—the chaotic everyday world that includes simple one-yolk eggs and musicians with all their extremities—might form only one section of such a table. All the other columns on our Peri-ODD-ic Table would be filled with the kinds of things people submitted to Robert Ripley.

Sequences and repetitions (like the "elevens" mentioned above) began to form a category that might also include people who named all their children alphabetically or alliteratively (as in "Dwight, Dwayne, Dwanda, Dworkin, and Dwella Dwindle of Dwyer, Delaware").

Dozens and dozens of duck-shaped sweet potatoes, hand-shaped carrots, dogs with heart-shaped spots, and cows with sevens on their forehead markings began to fall not only into their individual categories, but into a larger column of symbolic subjects that also included cross-shaped trees, snow, cacti, corn, cracks in mountains, and markings on fish. We couldn't resist the Holstein cow with the upside-down map of the Lower Peninsula of Michigan on its side, or the turtle Travis Robison found near Naples, Texas, whose shell looked like the face of a Chinese man.

A turtle marked with the face of a Chinaman, caught in Texarkana by TRAVIS ROBISON in 1933.

Another heading could include all the ironic submissions describing hens that insisted on laying their eggs in frying pans, all the turkeys that flew through butcher shop windows to rest their heads on chopping blocks, as well as all the ironic occupations like deaf phone operators, blind bowlers, bearded barbers, illiterate postmen, teetotaling barkeeps, swimming coaches who couldn't swim, and vegetarian hamburger cooks who had never tasted their own hamburgers. We didn't keep the Vegetarian Party presidential candidate, even though at eighty-six he was the oldest nominee ever to run.

A column of longevity items on the Peri-ODD-ic Table would list not only the folks who had smoked cigars all day every day since childhood and the shaving brushes that had given years of service, but razors and razor strops, hairbrushes, can openers, rolling pins, hairpins, collar buttons, socks, pens and pencils that all survived decades of such hard and constant use by their owners that they now provided them with incessant amazement. Wilbur Wilson of Tulsa sent Ripley a photo of a bicycle inner tube with 119 patches—and still holding air!

Readers would often hedge their bets when they sent items in for Ripley's consideration. "Not only do I have a razor blade that has served me faithfully for more than 52 years and never once been sharpened," wrote one anxious correspondent, "but also I have never gone a single day since age 14 without a carnation in my lapel."

Ripley fans sent in photos or descriptions of enough pocket watches found inside beef hearts, missing diamond rings discovered inside eggs, and lost keys that turned up inside Irish potatoes to set up an improbable Lost and Found Office. But they were run-of-the-mill Ripley correspondence fare, and we rarely set them aside. However, when Clinton Blume went swimming at Manhattan Beach in Brooklyn and bumped into his own monogrammed hairbrush floating in the surf—a hairbrush lost at sea when his ship was sunk by a German U-boat in 1918—now *that* was worth a pause to read the submission right through and a "Hey, come have a look at this!" to each other. Blume won the Grand Prize: an airplane and flying lessons in the 1932 Ripley's Contest with that entry. It didn't have a very exciting photograph, though, so back into the file it went, along with the letter from the man who scratched his initials onto a coin in California and had the same coin turn up in change in New York City five years later. . . .

There's often a fine line between the mundane and the truly miraculous, and whenever possible we opted for the latter—unless, of course, things were somehow miraculously mundane. Drinking a lot of water may not be miraculous in

and of itself, but when Edd Woolf downed almost six gallons and *still had room for a malt and sandwich* (see page 163), he crossed that line.

It was fun to think about a beer stein falling from the window of a third-floor tavern and landing on the sidewalk below without spilling a drop (or killing a passerby), but somehow the incident lacked that certain *je ne sais quoi* we were after for this book. If, say, it had dropped into the hands of a determined Prohibitionist and a photographer had captured the surprised and disgusted look, we might have included it here. Whenever possible, we wanted our lilies gilded!

The Ones That Got Away

A great deal of oddity failed to make it into this book because tastes, habits, social mores, and civil rights have changed since the heyday of Ripleymania. In the 1990s, for instance, when everyday wearing of hats is an exception rather than the norm, it's hard to share the thrill of all those who wrote Ripley to make the bold claim that they had gone more than a year without donning a cap, or else had traveled from Philadelphia to San Francisco *"without once putting on headgear!"* And even though Bub McKnight and Bill Shumacher thought their feat amazing enough to submit to Ripley, we weren't so impressed: they drove from Statesville, North Carolina, to Los Angeles *without a license plate* on their Model-A Ford! But this was back when there weren't so many patrolmen stalking the highways, either.

We drew other lines at racially or socially insensitive submissions, even though they might reflect in their own way the spirit of the times. We felt that kind of history should be studied, but not repeated. We'll admit to a wistful moment, though, when we considered using a photo of Methodist minister Hugh Williams of Ladora, Iowa, lifting his two-year-old daughter by the hair, but only because she was smiling. . . .

ELMER WILSON of Gorham, New Hampshire hedged his bets when sending in a photo to Ripley. On the one hand he is displaying a shaving brush which gave him 61 years of service. On the other hand he holds a potato that was "raised with only the sprout–no piece of potato was used."(November 19, 1947)

With few exceptions we have not included human or animal "freaks" in this book, though the files bulge with this type of material. For now, we decided to draw the line at Weng, the Human Unicorn, and Lentini, the Three-Legged Man, leaving other such human oddities for future prospectors to uncover and publish, and to limit the images of objects to a few weirdly animalized vegetables unless there happened to be people in the picture too.

A good portion of the Ripley Archives material is more verbal than visual, and because this is primarily a photo book we only hint at the riches with the inclusion of a selection of unusual names. It's enough, for instance, to state that the most expensive brand of perfume sold in the Soviet Union in 1952 was called "Stalin's Breath" without actually having to show you the bottle. We liked the picture of the sign outside the Washington, Indiana, cemetery that said

ANY THING
SO UNIVERSAL
AS DEATH
MUST BE
A BLESSING

and the wonderfully succinct epitaph cut into a rough gravestone that marked the spot where some unknown cowboy lay:

HE CALLED
BILL SMITH
A LIAR

But even though there were perfectly good pictures of these and thousands of other similar items, we left them aside here because as images they lacked that certain intersection of moment and event that makes the rest of the photographs in the book so memorable. We were after *show* as well as *tell.*

Any number of other books could have been done, and perhaps will be, by other workers who might come up with their own Taxonomy of the Odd. Ours is only a single core-sample extracted from an immense and vastly rich deposit, and the veins we worked would be extracted differently by others coming at them from different directions. Though our selection is unabashedly personal, we think our discoveries nevertheless hint at a precious and resilient spirit of human imagination that formed during hard times of economic and international struggle—a spirit still more valuable than gold.

What follows are some of the wonderful nuggets we found.

Robert Ripley: The Man and the Phenomenon

In an era marked by two world wars and the Great Depression, Robert Ripley's *Believe It or Not!* cartoons, books, and radio and television programs provided the public with a much-needed diversion from their daily routine. At the height of his extraordinary career, each installment of the daily cartoon was eagerly awaited by up to 80 million readers. The feature was syndicated in 300 newspapers and was translated into seventeen different languages. Additionally, his two books were best-sellers and his radio and television broadcasts were the most popular of the era. He received more mail than any other individual in history and earned the title of The Modern Marco Polo for his incessant globe-trotting. All this does not begin to describe the phenomenon Ripley created when, in 1918, he penned his first *Believe It or Not!* cartoon.

RIPLEY at the Temple of Maha Bodhi inspecting Buddha's footprints, 1936–37.

The Early Years

Robert LeRoy Ripley was born to parents of modest means in Santa Rosa, California, on Christmas Day in 1890. LeRoy, as he was then known, was always interested in drawing and in sports, particularly baseball. A self-taught artist, he published his first cartoon, entitled "The Village Bell Was Slowly Ringing," in *Life* magazine in 1908. The $8 check he received was enough to convince him that his future was in illustration. Ripley was an average student in high school but managed to persuade his teachers to allow him to illustrate the essays that other students were required to write. Young LeRoy Ripley also pitched baseball and achieved some local notoriety until an elbow injury put a stop to that ambition. Luckily Ripley's skills as an artist were very much intact. Through the efforts of a family friend, the fifteen-year-old Ripley landed a sports cartoonist job on the *San Francisco Bulletin* for $18 a week.

After two successful years there, he managed to land a better-paying job at the prestigious *San Francisco Chronicle*. During his four years in the City by the Bay, Ripley met Jack London and many other luminaries of the literary world and indulged his lifelong fascination with Chinese culture in Chinatown. In 1913 he asked for a slight raise from the *Chronicle* and was promptly fired. Undaunted, Ripley gathered his belongings and moved to New York with no job and little money.

RIPLEY'S first cartoon. December 19, 1918.

The New York of 1913 was a thriving metropolis. Ripley was instantly hired as a sports cartoonist for the *New York Globe* at $100 a week, which allowed him to send money back to his ailing mother in Santa Rosa until her death in 1915. Ripley gravitated to the numerous San Francisco transplants now working in New York. Restless after a year at his new job, the young cartoonist took his first trip abroad in 1914, with London, Paris, and Rome on the itinerary. There he visited the world's great museums and exposed himself to many new ideas.

Birth of *Believe It or Not!*

One day Ripley had a fast–approaching deadline but few ideas for his next day's cartoon. He had collected stories of unusual sports feats for quite some time with no particular idea of what to do with them. This time he grouped a selection of these sports oddities for his cartoon and at the top of the drawing lettered the words "Champs and Chumps." Upon seeing the cartoon, Ripley's editor said, "I like this idea, but these guys aren't really champs or chumps." Ripley then looked down at the pad, drew a line through the title, and wrote "Believe It or Not." His life was not to be the same after this cartoon appeared in the December 19, 1918, issue of the *Globe*.

Suddenly *Believe It or Not!* was a hit with the readers and there was a demand for more of these sports oddities. First it was a weekly, then a daily feature, then suddenly his little cartoon was syndicated in more than two dozen newspapers in the North-East. After six more years with the *Globe* Ripley signed on with the *New York Evening Post.*

Ripley in the Book World

Though Ripley had begun his career as a sports cartoonist, he soon realized that believe-it-or-nots could be found in all walks of life. The cartoon garnered scores of admirers, among them Max Schuster of the publishing firm Simon & Schuster, who tried to convince Ripley to put some of his most interesting *Believe It or Nots* between the covers of a book. Schuster even went so far as to dig up a few incredible items and send them to Ripley, but he shrugged off the idea and told Schuster that he was just a "two-cent man," the cost of a daily newspaper. Somehow, Schuster managed to cajole Ripley into assembling some of his personal favorites, and in 1929 the first *Ripley's Believe It or Not!* book was released to rave reviews. A second book followed two years later, then a third, omnibus edition, which was a combination of the first two books, was released in 1934. Millions of copies sold even though they were released during the dark years of the Depression.

RIPLEY'S contest submission (with cross-eyed cat).

The Hearst Connection

With his books climbing the best-seller charts, Ripley was on the way to becoming an institution. During the late 1920s, the newspaper business was dominated by King Features Syndicate, presided over by William Randolph Hearst. After seeing a copy of Ripley's first book, Hearst sent a two-word telegram to Joe Connoly, one of his operatives in New York: HIRE RIPLEY. Ripley was then in the enviable position of having several offers from rival syndicates, but after discussing the proposition with several of his associates, he decided to go with Hearst and signed with King Features Syndicate on July 9, 1929.

RIPLEY with local residents in Serrinia del Sabo, Panama, 1940.

King Features Syndicate brought *Believe It or Not!* into millions of households every day. Through an ingenious series of locally run contests, Ripley's cartoon began to generate huge mountains of correspondence. Everyone wanted in on the act. Ripley received more than 3,500 letters per day, or a million letters per year, during the thirties and forties. During one contest Ripley received 2,500,000 letters in fourteen days! This explosion of interest forced Ripley to hire a team of secretaries just to sort and edit the incoming mail. Now that the feature was being carried in dozens of foreign newspapers as well, Ripley had to hire translators to help him reach his worldwide audience. The colossal distribution network of King Features Syndicate newspapers was one of the key ingredients to Ripley's success.

The Modern Marco Polo

Ripley stayed close to home during World War I but in 1920 took his first trip to South America. He returned there in 1924 and wrote a column for the *New York Post* called "Rambles 'Round South America." After his first encounter with the Orient in 1923, China became his adopted country. A dedicated Orientalist, for a brief period he even signed his cartoons "Rip Li." The cartoonist had already made many trips, but after he signed with King Features Syndicate and became known as The Modern Marco Polo (a phrase attributed to the Duke of Windsor), all of his travels were highly publicized.

While his newspaper feature was fast becoming one of the most popular of the era, Ripley took advantage of the

Human unicorn. (June 10, 1945)

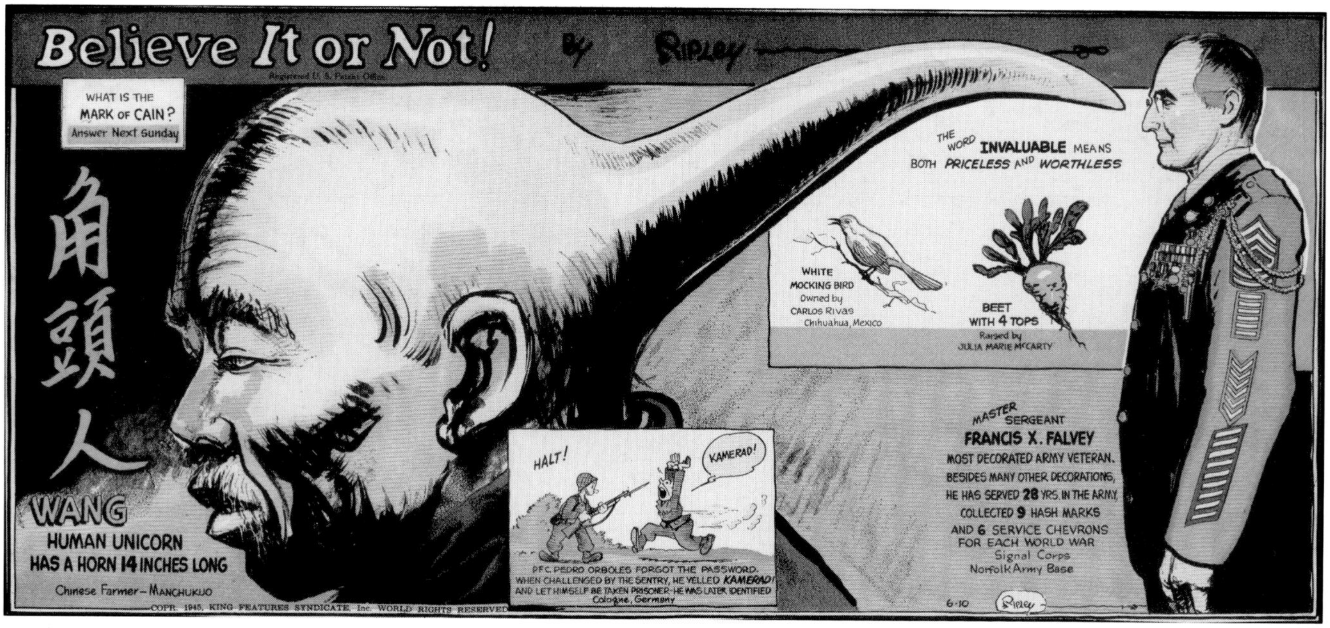

opportunity to travel in search of adventure—and, of course, to hunt for new material for the cartoon. Travel thereafter dominated Ripley's life, and with his passport stamped by 201 countries, he became the most widely traveled man of his time. As befitted a man of his celebrity, he traveled by luxury steamer and airplanes, but, as a connoisseur of the unusual, he also straddled camels and donkeys and floated by gufa boat. Because of his association with Hearst, Ripley had virtually unlimited wealth at his disposal. He traveled to some of the most primitive and remote corners of the globe in search of ever stranger wonders and curiosities. The more remote and inaccessible the location, the more Ripley enjoyed going there.

Many of his comings and goings were celebrated with lavish feasts and parties. Fifteen hundred people attended one soiree at the Waldorf-Astoria ballroom, where the dinner menu was penned in fifteen different languages.

Despite the economic hardships pounding the United States during the 1930s, Ripley weathered the Depression with an annual income of approximately $500,000. However, his success had not blinded him to the disparity between rich and poor. After his visit to the Soviet Union in 1934, Ripley wrote a scathing indictment of the Communist government and called the country "a great poorhouse," where thousands of citizens were starving and the living conditions were unbearable. Since his columns were carried by the largest newspaper syndicate in the world, the Communist government branded Ripley *persona non grata,* forbidding his return. Ripley, always a fierce patriot, donated his time freely to worthy causes—selling war bonds or raising morale at home after the outbreak of World War II.

Famous for his constant globe-trotting, Ripley became a member of the Circumnavigator's Club, and the Royal Geographic Society made him a Fellow. To commemorate his obsession with travel he had a giant compass embedded in the floor of his Mamaroneck home that indicated the mileage to various faraway destinations. In his thirty-five years on the road Ripley traversed a distance equal to eighteen revolutions around the planet. On one expedition he crossed two continents and covered over 24,000 miles from New York to Cairo and back. The modes of travel for this journey included 15,000 miles by air, 8,000 by ship, and over 1,000 miles by camel, donkey, and horse.

RIPLEY cartoon with Charles Schulz illustration.

Anvil lifter. (October 27, 1946)

Evolution of the Cartoon

Ripley's bold style of cartooning spurred many imitators. None, however, ever got very far. In Ripley's case it was not only the drawings that captivated viewers, but the stories behind them as well. One gigantic advantage Ripley had over his competition was that his readers kept him supplied with more material than he could possibly use. Readers were constantly trying to one-up a feat they had seen in the cartoon, and in this sense it was not merely a reflection of the society, it actually fed on itself. An example would be the case of a waiter named Mr. Hugo (page 44), who could carry eleven cups of coffee with one hand. After seeing this feat chronicled in the Ripley cartoon, Charles Russell (page 45) carried twelve cups of coffee in one hand while holding his sister over his head with the other. While he was wearing ice skates. This kind of sportsmanship was part and parcel of Ripleymania.

Ripley's admirers and cartoon hopefuls sent him all kinds of documentary evidence of their particular claims to fame, but Ripley preferred photographs over all other forms of proof. Most of his cartoons were drawn directly from these photographs. In the days before the photocopier, Ripley lightly covered the back of the photograph with graphite from a pencil. He would then flip the print over, lay it on a sheet of paper, and firmly outline the figure directly on the surface of the picture. When he lifted up the photo, there would be a faint outline traced by the graphite on the blank paper below for him to use as the basis for the cartoon. As a commercial illustrator Ripley depended on photographic documentation, both as evidence and as visual catalyst.

Occasionally, Ripley fans would send in one of their own drawings to entice the master. Fledgling cartoonist Charles Schulz, who later created *Charlie Brown* and *Peanuts,* first appeared in print in a 1937 Ripley cartoon. Schulz, who submitted a drawing of his dog, was twelve years old at the time. The dog was the model for the now famous Snoopy character in Schulz's wildly successful cartoon.

Color postcard
from the Chicago Odditorium, 1933.

FRANÇOIS RUSSELL, removes nails with his teeth.

Odditoriums

At the 1933 Century of Progress World's Fair in Chicago Ripley unveiled his first Odditorium. This landmark exhibition contained posters of *Believe It or Not!* cartoons, shrunken heads, instruments of torture, medieval chastity belts, and other strange artifacts from around the world. Living performers served as proof of some of his more colorful cartoon personalities. This type of museum was a direct descendant of P. T. Barnum's American Museum in New York City of the 1840s. One of P. T. Barnum's most famous and celebrated hoaxes involved the Fiji Mermaid, wherein prospective museum-goers saw an artist's rendition of the beautiful, buxom maiden-fish of legend and lore, yet upon entering found a monkey's head clumsily joined to the body of a fish. The gambit netted Barnum a national reputation as a showman and an ace promoter, along with boosting the coffers of the American Museum. When Robert Ripley purchased a Fiji Mermaid that was said to have once been owned by P. T. Barnum, the historical links and natural affinities between these two born showmen were clearly demonstrated.

RIPLEY and friend with the Fiji Mermaid, New York Odditorium, 1939.

Visitors fainted by the dozens at the Chicago Odditorium, yet it was one of the most heavily visited of all of the World's Fair attractions during the two-year run of the Century of Progress. More than two million people passed through the Odditorium doors in 1933. Inside they witnessed contortionists, fireproof people, razor blade eaters, sword swallowers, magicians, eye poppers, and other live attractions. Ripley disdained the term *freaks* and insisted his employees refer to unusual people instead as *oddities*. The showing in Chicago was so successful, Ripley soon opened other Odditoriums in Cleveland, Dallas, San Diego, San Francisco, and New York. By the time his New York Odditorium opened on Broadway in 1939, Ripley had toned down some of the more extreme acts from the Chicago days. Fewer people fainted anyway.

26

JOE LAURELLO, Head Turner.

LYDIA MCPHERSON,
The Longest Red Hair in the World.

SINGLEE, The Fireproof Hindu.

HABU KOLLER, The Iron Tongue Man.

THE GREAT OMI, The World's Most Heavily Tattooed Person.

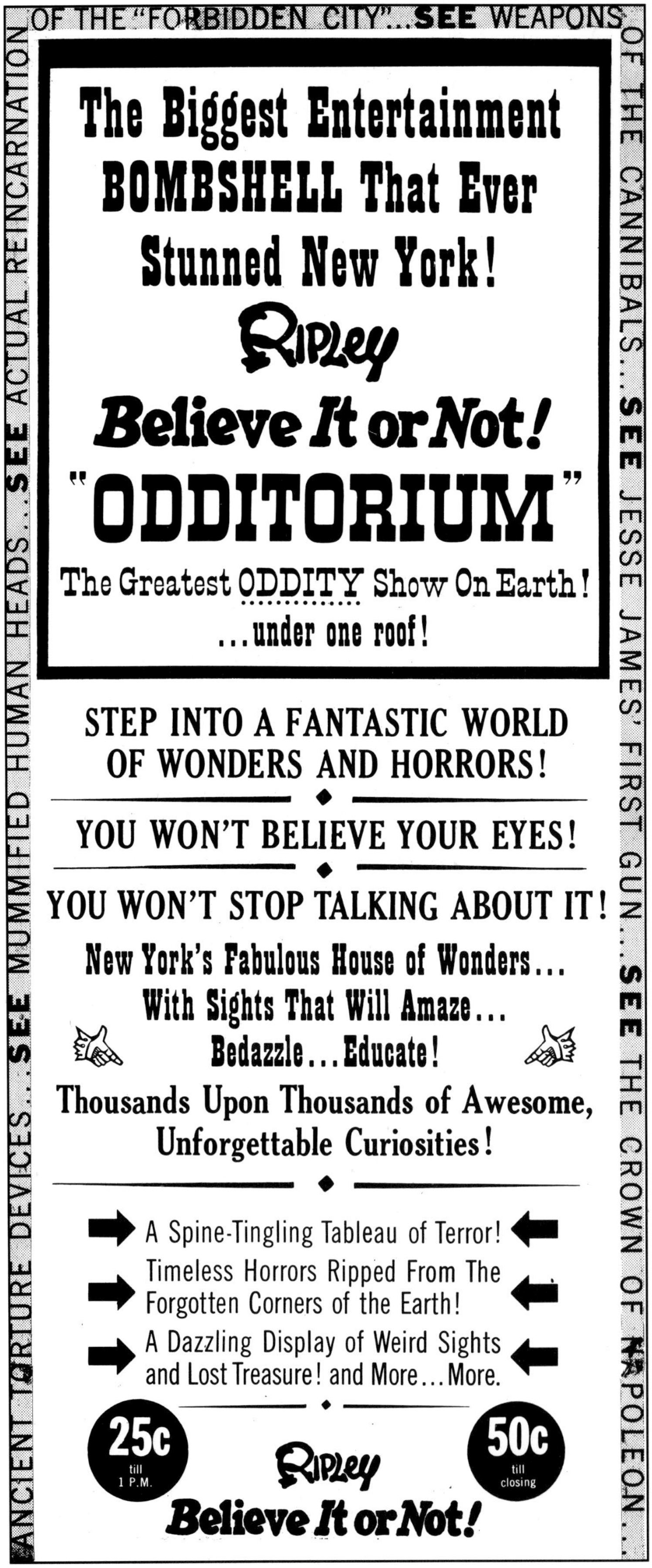

Handbill from New York Odditorium.

Ripley, the Unlikely Broadcast Pioneer

Surprisingly shy in public and afflicted with a slight stutter, Robert Ripley nevertheless became a pioneer in the field of radio and television broadcasting. His first radio broadcast was in 1930 when he delivered a few believe-it-or-nots on a show called the *Collier Hour*. Three years later and with several modifications, the radio version of *Believe It or Not!* expanded to include guest stars and featured a live band. Ripley had been strenuously coached in diction by his producer/director Doug Storer. The *Believe It or Not!* broadcasts were among the most popular of their day, attracting numerous sponsors eager to take advantage of Ripley's popularity. The radio program produced a number of scoops during a time before instantaneous news. One of these was the story of "Wrong Way" Corrigan. This fearless young East Coast pilot wanted to fly across the Atlantic but knew that the authorities would never grant him permission. Corrigan filed a flight plan stating the West Coast as his final destination, yet he ended up in Dublin, Ireland, where Ripley interviewed him: "A fellow can't help it if he gets mixed up, can he?"

Robert Ripley, Birmingham, Alabama, 1948 (with radio equipment).

Some of the other remote pickups were remarkable for their rarity and for the technological accomplishments they illustrated. For example, one radio program set up a two-way link with parachutist Jack Huber, who gave a blow-by-blow description of a two-mile free-fall plunge before opening his parachute. Other unusual broadcasting locations included the North Pole, the Cave of the Winds under Niagara Falls, Carlsbad Caverns in New Mexico, and Nassau in the Bahamas, where the Duke of Windsor gave his first Western Hemisphere radio interview. One of the broadcasts originated from a twelve-foot canvas boat shooting the rapids of the Colorado River at night. Oddly enough, the announcer on board was a Phoenix-based department store owner named Barry Goldwater.

Earlier Ripley radio programs originated from a small studio where Ripley and his producer dramatized a *believe-it-or-not!* and brought to life the incredible stories behind some of the cartoons. The programs often featured Odditorium performers who were brought into the studio for interviews. In 1940, *Radio Guide* magazine rated Ripley's program as "consistently the most interesting and thrilling on the air."

In 1931 and 1932, Ripley contracted to make a series of twenty-six short talking movie features with Warner Brothers–Vitaphone. In these brief film clips, presented along with newsreels and previews in movie theaters across the United States, Ripley interviewed some of his *Believe It or Not!* personalities or explained some of the more elaborate stories behind his cartoons. Today, these shorts seem amateurish and contrived, but at the time they were among the most popular entertainments available. One of Ripley's favorite ploys was to challenge a popularly held notion. One such *believe-it-or-not!* rested on a rather spurious distinction, but Ripley was correct when he claimed that "Buffalo Bill never shot a buffalo in his life." The animal that roamed the American plains was the bison.

Ripley insured his place in history books when he proclaimed in a 1929 cartoon that the United States did not have an official national anthem. Thousands of readers wrote in response, and Ripley referred their letters to Congress. As a result of the cartoon, "The Star-Spangled Banner" was officially adopted as the national anthem of the United States.

In the early 1940s Ripley also participated in the embryonic days of television. At the time there were only a few thousand television sets in New York City, and the primitive Nielsen-type rating system was conducted with postcards. The war effort drew attention away from this new entertainment technology, but when peace returned Ripley jumped back into television with both feet. The *Believe It or Not!*

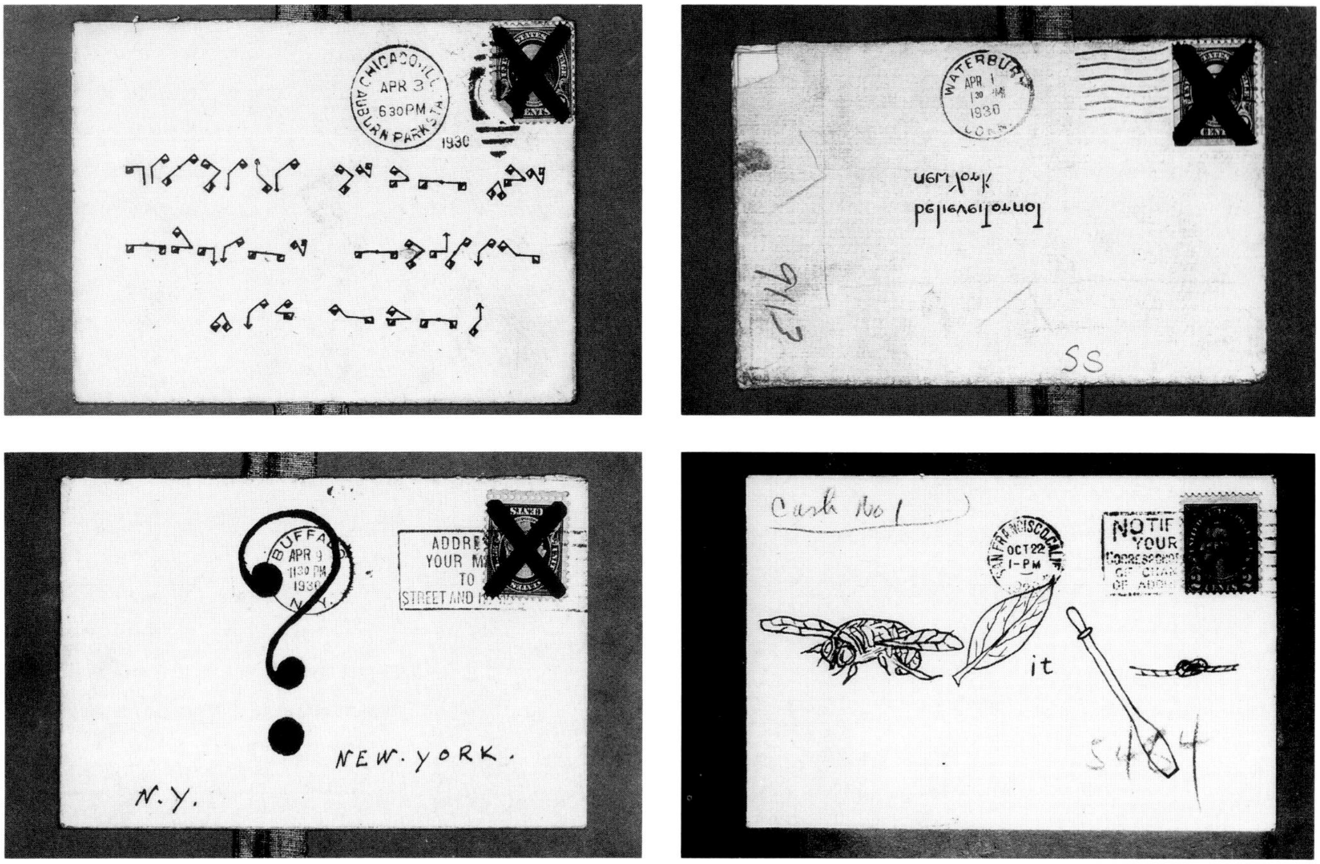

A selection of RIPLEY'S mail.

television series was also one of the most popular of the era, covering much the same ground as his radio broadcasts.

The highlights of Ripley's broadcasting career include several firsts: he was the first to send a cartoon by radio (from London to the *New York Tribune* in 1927); the first to send a drawing by telephone (from Chicago to New York in 1927); the first to broadcast to a nationwide network from mid-ocean (in 1931); the first to broadcast from Australia to New York, from aboard the *Mariposa* (in 1932); the first to broadcast from Buenos Aires to New York (in 1933); and the first to broadcast to every nation in the world simultaneously, assisted by a corps of linguists who translated his message into various tongues (in 1934).

Ripley's Mailbag

Ripley maintained that he would furnish proof of any of his claims if the doubter would send in a stamped envelope. Some of his voluminous mail was from people eager to prove him wrong, but most of it contained suggestions for future cartoons. People sent Ripley photographs, maps, charts, drawings, notarized napkins, and sworn affidavits pertaining to all manner of subjects, attempting to provide conclusive proof of items that would pique the cartoonist's curious mind. Some people went to extremes to provide iron-clad evidence. Many of the verification forms in the Ripley Archives were signed by police chiefs, judges, clergy, or, when absolute proof was required, by bartenders.

The *Believe It or Not!* phenomenon spawned its own fads. One of these was to see who could come up with the most obscure address on their envelope and still have Ripley receive it. There were some truly spectacular examples, including those addressed to him in Braille, wigwag, Morse code, semaphore, and in backwards, upside-down English. Sometimes the envelope would be addressed simply to the World's Biggest Liar. Many had only a squiggly (ripply) line drawn on the front, or there were those who put a photograph or drawing of Ripley on the envelope. One of Ripley's favorite specimens in the unusual mail category was a stamp from Yokohama, Japan, with only the word *Ripley* written on the back, which arrived despite its lack of an envelope.

The *Mon Lei*—an original watercolor by RIPLEY himself.

So prevalent was this fad that the U.S. Postmaster General Walter F. Brown issued a decree on April 30, 1930:

Mail to Robert Ripley will not be delivered if the address is incomplete or indecipherable. Such letters hereafter will be either returned to the sender or sent to the dead letter office. Postal clerks have had to devote too much time recently deciphering freak letters intended for Ripley.

Wayne Harbour of Bedford, Iowa, became so obsessed by the *Believe It or Not!* craze that he spent all his spare time trying to disprove Ripley. For twenty-six years this persnickety postmaster wrote a letter a day challenging at least one claim in the daily cartoon. As of 1970, he had written 22,708 letters to people highlighted in the cartoon and had received 10,363 replies. None of the responses Harbour received contradicted Ripley's claims.

Obsessive Collector

Ripley surrounded himself with objects of his liking. Whether he was at his palatial home in Mamaroneck, New York, called BION (the acronym for Believe It or Not), his sumptuous apartment on Central Park, or his beach estate called Hi-Mount in Palm Beach, Florida, Ripley's personal collection of "curioddities" were in abundance everywhere. His biographer, Bob Considine, claimed that Ripley confused "tonnage with taste" when it came to outfitting his houses. There did seem to be a great many massive objects in all of Ripley's homes. Without question, Ripley's most prized possession was a Chinese junk called the *Mon Lei*, a Foochow riverboat that had been confiscated by the Japanese when they invaded China in the 1930s. In typical Ripley fashion, the ship was modified with a gigantic engine that worked at cross-purposes with the wind-filled sails. There were a number of other vessels in the Ripley fleet: an Alaskan kayak, a gufa boat made of woven reeds in the shape of a giant round basket, a Seminole Indian dugout canoe, and an assortment of more conventional rowboats, but the *Mon Lei* was the skipper's pride. Ripley used the ship both for relaxing and as a floating advertisement. He could be seen sailing this unusual craft near his home on Long Island Sound and occasionally up the Hudson River. The *Mon Lei* was one of Ripley's favorite places to entertain his many guests. He

greeted statesmen, celebrities, and common folk aboard this floating anachronism. And what better way to announce the arrival of the creator of *Believe It or Not!*

Besides boats and houses, Ripley had dozens of other interests as a collector. In the 1930s it was still possible for a person of means to travel to distant lands and bring back cultural treasures, which Ripley did, self-consciously living out the myth of the Great White Explorer. He had collections of money from around the globe, Fijian war clubs, Tibetan altar bowls made from the skulls of Buddhist saints, Japanese armor, Samurai swords, and Jivaro shrunken heads, to list but a few of his holdings. Many of these objects later found their way into the Odditoriums, but some stayed in his personal collections at home. One of his favorite conversation starters at BION was his stein and tankard collection, which numbered in the hundreds and included one that was made from the tooth socket of a walrus! Ripley delighted in showing his possessions to visitors, whether in his own homes or in the Odditoriums. No matter how consumed he was in tending to his sprawling enterprise, he could still sparkle as he wondered aloud whether the hair on the shrunken heads continued to grow *after* he acquired them.

Ripley with giant cigar, Brazil, 1923.

The Legacy

Robert LeRoy Ripley died of a heart attack on May 27, 1949, at the age of fifty-nine, but his legacy is still very much with us. The expression "believe it or not!" has entered the language and has a universally understood meaning, and an organization that bears his name is still in existence and continues to publish the books and cartoon features he created. He is buried in the Odd Fellows Cemetery in Santa Rosa, California.

Alexandre Patty ascending a staircase by cranial hopping. (February 15, 1931)

The golden age of Robert Ripley was during the 1930s and '40s, when his popularity was unrivaled and the phrase "There's one for Rip" was on everyone's lips. Ripley succeeded in creating an American institution that celebrated the uniqueness and diversity of the human spirit. He employed every medium available to tell of the unusual people he had met, places he had seen, and phenomena he had witnessed. King Features Syndicate kept the cartoon going in the style of the master for many years, and today it is produced in-house by Ripley Entertainment Inc. It continues to appear regularly in nearly two hundred newspapers. The Ripley's organization is active and thriving, with new museums opening each year. The collection of over 8,000 objects that Ripley amassed has been dispersed to the various Believe It or Not! museums throughout the world, which continue to attract millions of new fans annually. That the interest in the life and activities of Robert Ripley continues speaks of the universal appeal of the phenomenon he created. Today there are numerous popular television shows that mine the same mother lode that Ripley did, while many of the so-called tabloid newspapers now present items that would fall into the "or not" rather than the "believe it" column.

One of the most enduring legacies left by Robert Ripley is his insistence on the authenticity and verification of the facts presented in the cartoon. His chief of research, Norbert Pearlroth, worked six days a week for fifty-two years at the New York Public Library checking and double-checking the source materials for accuracy. The man who was frequently called the World's Biggest Liar was in fact a stickler for details. The hallmark of the *Believe It or Not!* phenomenon was that the basic outline of these outrageous claims was true, and that Ripley could invariably furnish some sort of proof, frequently in the form of an actual photograph of the oddity he described. More often than not, seeing is believing.

A Delicate Balance

"Etiquette requires us to admire the human race."

Mark Twain

Joe Horowitz could balance an 18-pound saber on his nose. Billed as the Man with the Iron Nose, Horowitz performed his spectacular act in theaters near his native Los Angeles. **(December 21, 1934)**

Gravity seemed to be no obstacle for Hurley, WISCONSIN'S **ELI VICELLIO,** who **could lift a table and chair** weighing 70 pounds **with his teeth. (March 25, 1947)**

Five- and seven-year-old **PATRICIA AND GERALDINE ELLERT** of Baltimore, MARYLAND, **perform an outstanding feat of agility and strength.** Geraldine is the "understander" and Patricia is the top mount. **(September 4, 1941)**

Twenty-one-year-old **ALICE PENFOLD lifts her sister Mary** on a stool **by her teeth only.** The sisters were from Bury, ENGLAND. **(December 21, 1953)**

Adrian C. Fox of Park River, North Dakota, shown here **lifting a 145-pound mandolinist** in a chair supported by his head and mouth. **(July 5, 1936)**

JACKIE DEL RIO chewed not only his steak but the table as well! And not only his own table but the next table and all the chairs! **Two tables and six chairs altogether.** Aside from merely lifting ordinary furniture by his molars, the five-foot-tall Chicagoan was also able to lift a person seated in a chair. **(February 17, 1938)**

Lawn mower hoister **ROBERT DOTZAUER** of Lisbon, IOWA, although crippled in one leg, **could balance three heavy iron mowers on his chin.** Total weight of lawn mowers: 150 pounds. Total weight of Dotzauer: 145 pounds. **(November 12, 1953)**

Calvert
Chicago

James Paul, The Greek Titan of Brooklyn, New York, **could lift six persons totaling 735 pounds with his teeth.** He claimed to have had a "weak condition" of the teeth for three years for which he visited a quack doctor in Cypress, Greece, who gave him a special preparation paste that had dramatic results. Favorite foods: cabbage heads and carrots. Height five foot six, weight 140 pounds. **(August 14, 1951)**

South Chicago "Y" physical instructor **Charles Russell lifted two ukelele-playing belles** to prove that music could tame but not weaken the savage beast. **(May 18, 1939)**

CHARLES C. RUSSELL
Y.M.C.A.
ICE SKATING AND BARBELL INSTRUCTOR
LIFTING 265 LB'S.
CALUMET STUDIO.

Squad of men standing on a Douglas fir plywood board at the Elliott Bay Mill Company in SEATTLE. **Only a quarter-inch thick, the plyboard supported their combined weight of 1,833 pounds** without splitting. **(November 1, 1931)**

A magnetic pulley holds a man by the iron nails in his shoes (with co-workers dangling from an iron bar) at Dings Magnetic Separator Company in MILWAUKEE. **(May 4, 1937)**

DINGS
MAGNETIC SEPARATOR
Co.
U.S.A.

Mr. Hugo, an employee of Brown's Restaurant in New York City, here shown **carrying eight cups of coffee with one hand.** Hugo later topped his own feat by toting ten cups in one hand. He was also able to take orders for twenty-five sandwiches at one time without writing them down and serve them all correctly. **(August 13, 1931)**

"PHYSICAL PERFECTIONIST" **CHARLES RUSSELL** received quite a bit of mail after his appearance in Ripley's cartoon on May 18, 1939, prompting him to try even harder for another claim to fame. Russell saw the BION cartoon about Mr. Hugo, who was able to carry eight cups of coffee with one hand, and figured if he **hoisted his sister in one hand and twelve cups of coffee in the other—on ice skates—**he, too, could achieve another entry in Ripley's feature. His logic proved infallible. **(February 21, 1942)**

Clayton's Café in Tyler, TEXAS, boasted that waitress **BLANCHE LOWE** could **carry twenty-three coffee cups in one hand. (April 9, 1940)**

Jeannette, Pa;
June 9, 1931.

Mr. Ripley-: If the feat of Charles Gordon (Holding 17 tennis balls) is worthy of your Believe It Or Not Column Compare it to the two photographs I submit to you.

I am still watching and waiting for results, concerning the two submissions made by Harold Cook, Dec. 27, 1930. The picking up and holding of 18 regulation sized base balls, or 9 in each hand, held with palms down. Also the picking up and holding of 20 pocket billiard balls, or 10 in each hand, held with palms down.

Respectfully Yours,
(The World's Champion)
?

Julius B. Shuster,
#700 Magee Ave.

Julius B. Schuster, card sharp and world's champion "Pickup Artist," **held twenty billiard balls in one hand** in Jeanette, Pennsylvania. Schuster was one of Ripley's favorite Odditorium performers, and Ripley frequently featured his manual dexterity skills not only in the cartoon, but also on *Believe It or Not!* radio and television programs. Other stunts included picking up and **holding twenty-five tennis balls and twenty baseballs,** and most difficult of all, picking up from a flat surface and holding ten billiard balls in each hand in such a way that the hands could be turned **in any position, even upside down. (July 6, 1931)**

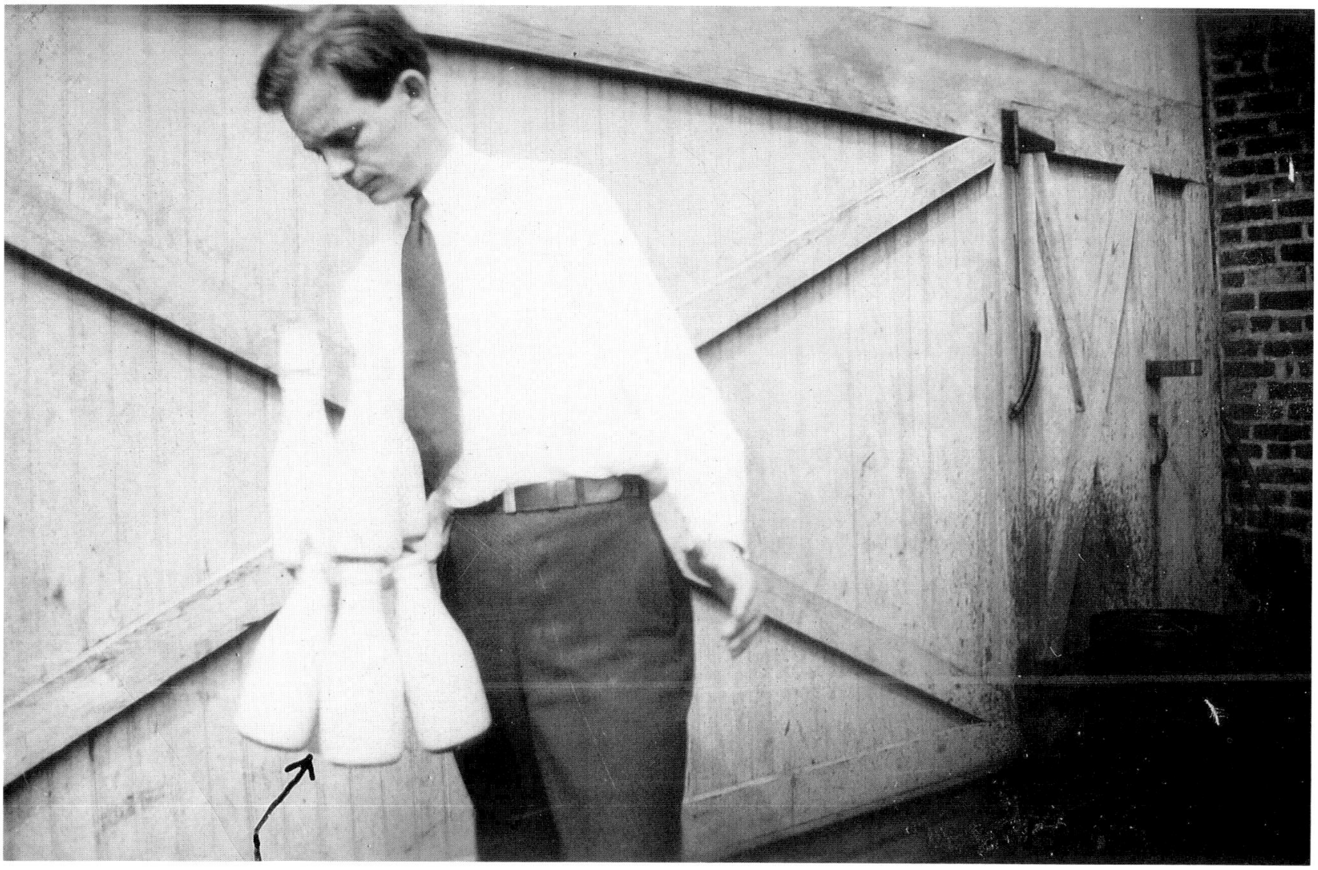

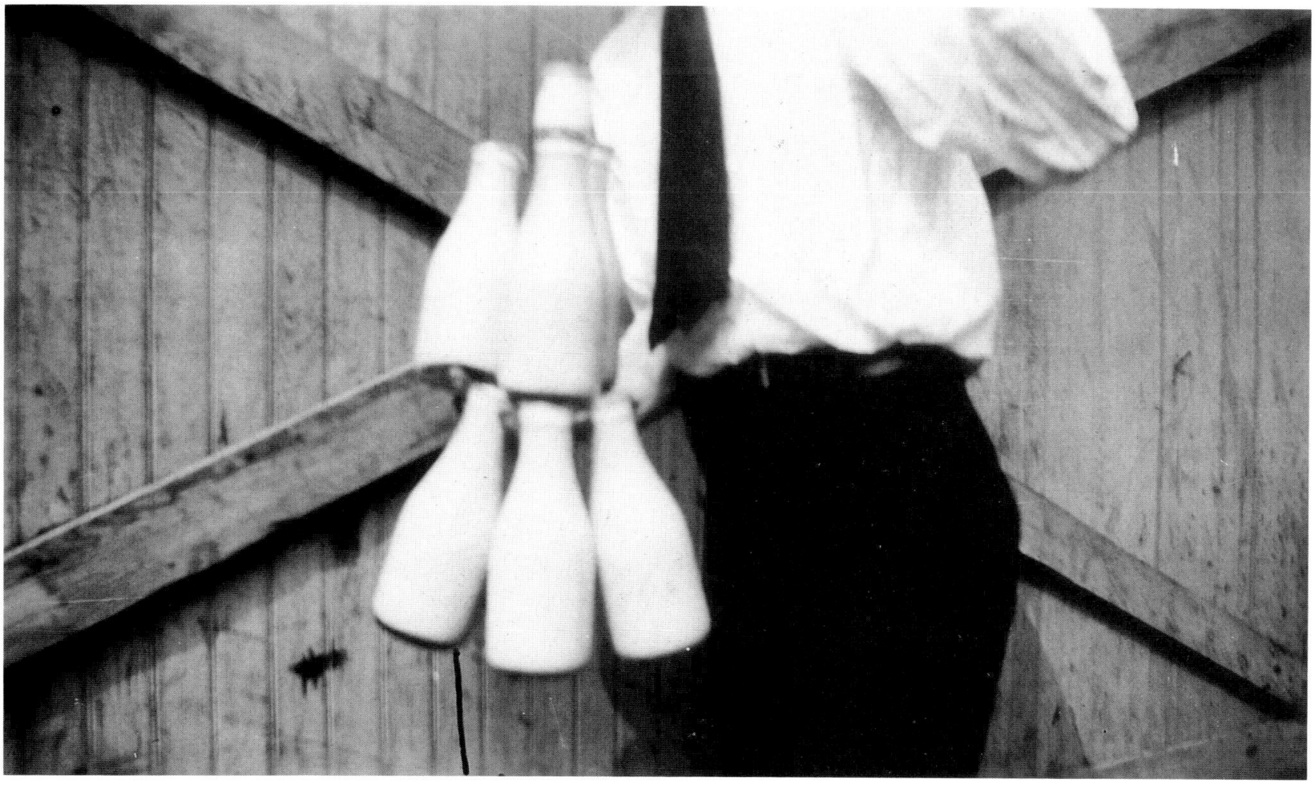

JOSEPH E. WIEDENMAYER, JR., of Bloomfield, NEW JERSEY, developed the unique specialty of **lifting eight full quarts of milk with one hand. (September 14, 1932)**

For a man who had not used a toothbrush, toothpaste, or tooth powder in over twenty years, **John M. Hernic** sure had good teeth. Here he is shown **lifting a 180-pound man** with little effort. **(December 8, 1935)**

ROBERT FERN of Dallas, TEXAS, could **balance a quarter on his nose for half a minute. (June 28, 1933)**

Dislocationists, Contortionists, and Elastic People

"Anatomy is destiny."

Sigmund Freud

Henry D. Lewis, the oldest person in St. Augustine, Florida (itself the oldest city in the United States), **at age ninety-five proved he was still spry.** He said his ability spoke well for the Florida climate, where he had wintered for the last twenty-nine years. **(June 3, 1936)**

HENRY D. LEWIS
95 YEARS YOUNG

Hats off to acrobat **Dad A. T. Brown, who climbed a forty-foot pole** in Grand Junction, Colorado, **on his eightieth birthday.** As if that weren't enough, he lowered himself down headfirst! **(August 7, 1934)**

Perry L. Biddle of DeFuniack Springs, Florida, **hoists himself up into a Human Flag** position on his **ninetieth birthday. (October 30, 1936)**

Sixty-four-year-old Ed Thardo performed this contortion feat in Handley, Texas. He was the contortionist for the Harley Sadler Traveling Show for many years. **(March 4, 1934)**

Champion of the Freearm Planche, **sixty-five-year-old W. H. Mering challenged anyone else in the world** to perform this stunt. Mr. Mering taught a hand-balancing class at the Hollywood Y.M.C.A. **(October 11, 1938)**

ROBERT AITKEN of SAN FRANCISCO could **take off his hat with a doubled-back arm. (November 22, 1938)**

F. VELEZ CAMPOS, dislocationist, strikes a peculiar pose in Fortuna, PUERTO RICO. (**September 23, 1933)**

Is he coming or going? Demetrio Ortiz of Los Angeles performs the unusual feat of **twisting his body 180 degrees. (August 12, 1932)**

MAY RUTH BASS of Jacksonville, FLORIDA, said, **"I have been kissing the floor, kicking my forehead with either foot, and shaking my hips** [independently of other body parts] **all my life."** What's more, she wrote Ripley to say she could sing a song while kissing the floor, change flat tires and fan belts, and drive a stick shift. **(November 23, 1937)**

Due to a strange **twist** of fate, **AVERY TUDOR** of NEW YORK CITY was able to **turn his feet around backwards. (December 15, 1936)**

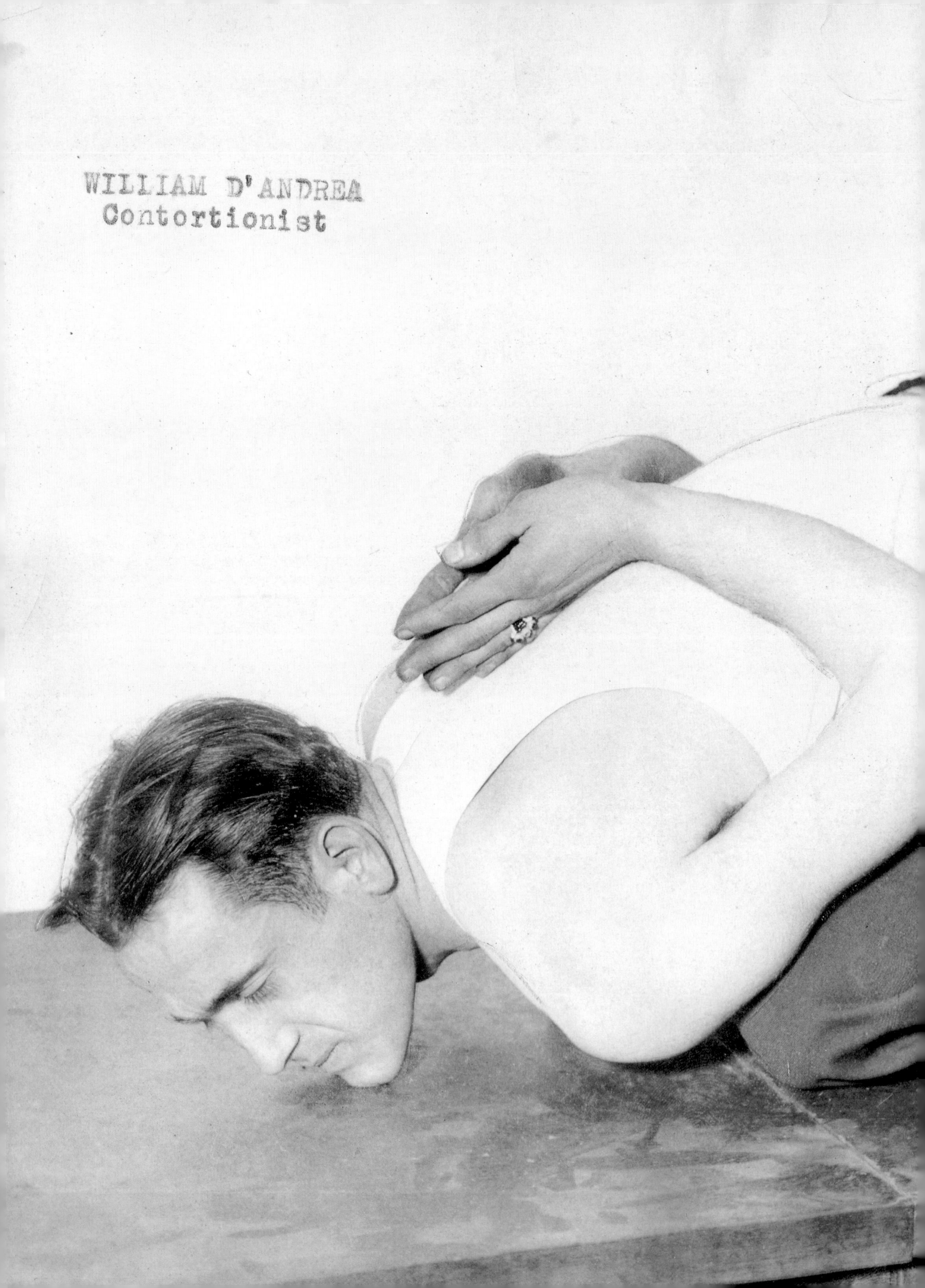
WILLIAM D'ANDREA
Contortionist

Contortionist **Edward Lucas** of Chico, California, **takes a deep bow.** The young dancer attributed his ability to "loose hips and extremely stretched muscles." **(January 9, 1934)**

William D'Andrea, contortionist of Waterbury, Connecticut, could put his feet in his pockets while standing, in addition to his **unusual praying position. (February 14, 1935)**

THE ONLY MAN IN THE
WORLD WHO CAN SIT
ON A GLASS 2½ INCHES
ACROSS THE TOP

The Great Johnson, a.k.a. The Silent Entertainer, was able to **balance himself on an ordinary 2 1/2-inch-wide drinking tumbler** in addition to performing countless other contortionist poses to dazzle the masses. **(November 6, 1940)**

Los Angeles dancer **Miss Renée DeLue** and her partner, **Ruby Dale,** demonstrate their version of **a Human Belt.** Appreciative audiences put them **on a pedestal** for many years. **(August 29, 1946)**

Moyne Mullin of Berkeley, California, worked for five years to perfect this **funny-bone balance.** Her entire weight is supported by her elbows. **(January 25, 1948)**

A direct descendant of the Chevalier Troupe of acrobats, **LORRAIN CHEVALIER** of Philadelphia, PENNSYLVANIA, **was actually able to sit on her own head!** The family claims that in 200 years only one person per generation of Chevaliers was suited to this type of work. **(October 24, 1937)**

JACQUELINE TERRY of Montgomery, ALABAMA, performing her **unusual jaw-balancing act** at age seventeen in PHILADELPHIA. Rumor had it that her father was an orthodontist. **(October 5, 1948)**

ALMA YNCLAN, child contortionist of Tampa, FLORIDA, appeared in Ripley cartoons several times, performing such stunts as The Living Cross, **standing on her own back,** and the like. **(April 5, 1937)**

HAMMERS, NAILS, NEEDLES, AND PINS

"Democracy is based on the conviction that there are extraordinary possibilities in ordinary people."

HARRY EMERSON FOSDICK

LEO KONGEE of PITTSBURGH **could drive 60-penny nails into his nose** and stick hatpins into his body without discomfort. He traveled around the country for twenty-three years performing his PAINLESS WONDER act in mud shows before joining the Odditorium Show in 1933. He also **held his socks up with tacks driven into his legs** or with safety pins and thread sewn through his flesh. He sewed buttons onto his arms and tongue and put skewers through his cheeks and nose.
His friends called him PROFESSOR KONGEE or sometimes PROFESSOR NESBITT. **(September 2, 1934)**

Richmond, VIRGINIA'S own Peruvian fakir, **JOSÉ FERNANDEZ,** could swallow safety razor blades and **drive a 20-penny nail into his head up to the hilt** (if nails have hilts). This feat was witnessed by the *Richmond News Leader* staff and was submitted as their entry in a national Ripley contest.
(July 9, 1932)

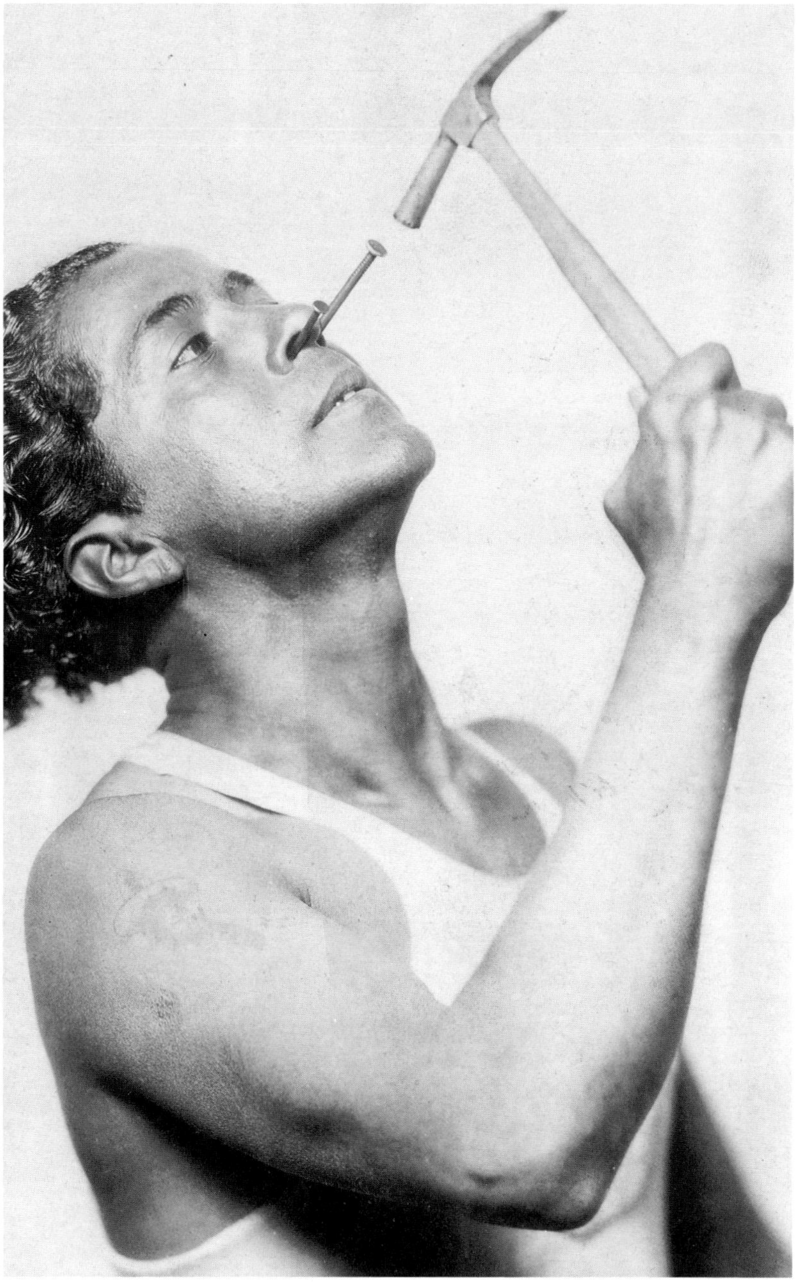

AUGUST L. SCHMOLT of SAN FRANCISCO **banged his biceps with a four-pound hammer daily for forty years** without ever bruising or blackening his skin. No reason was given for this unique pastime, but Schmolt said that he was a "performer" in his youth.
(August 15, 1944)

MRS. JAKE HAMON of Ardmore, OKLAHOMA, had her husband's diamond cuff links made into **a pin that she wore pierced through her throat.** She wore it this way continuously while, presumably, Mr. Hamon's cuffs went linkless.
(December 15, 1933)

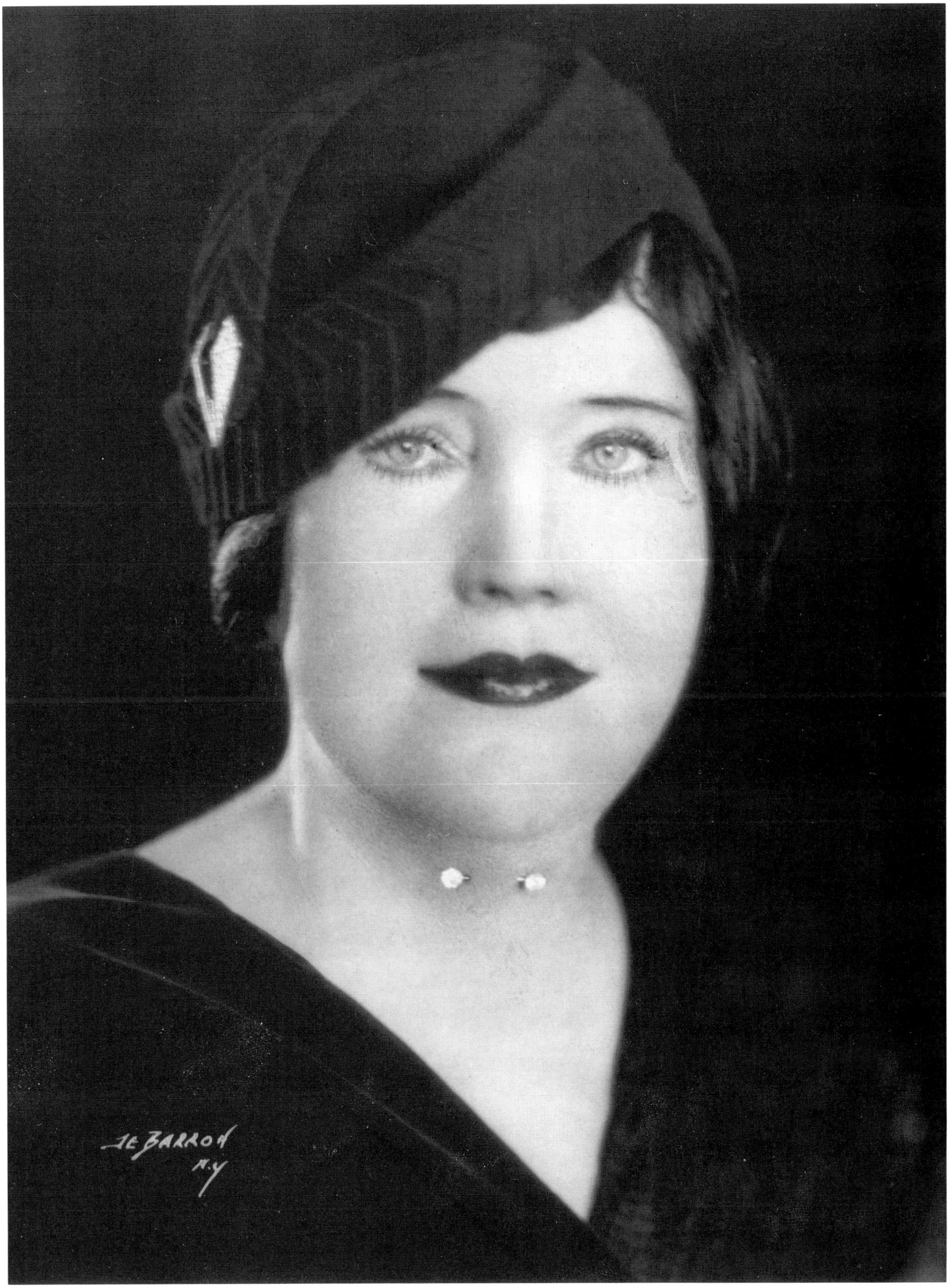
DE BARRON
N.Y.

CORDELIA STEWART of San Jose, CALIFORNIA, **swallowed a needle as a young woman.** Several years later, **her firstborn child, Julia, produced the same needle from her thigh at six months of age.** The biggest question in this mystery of the migrating needle is how it got swallowed in the first place. **(March 17, 1941)**

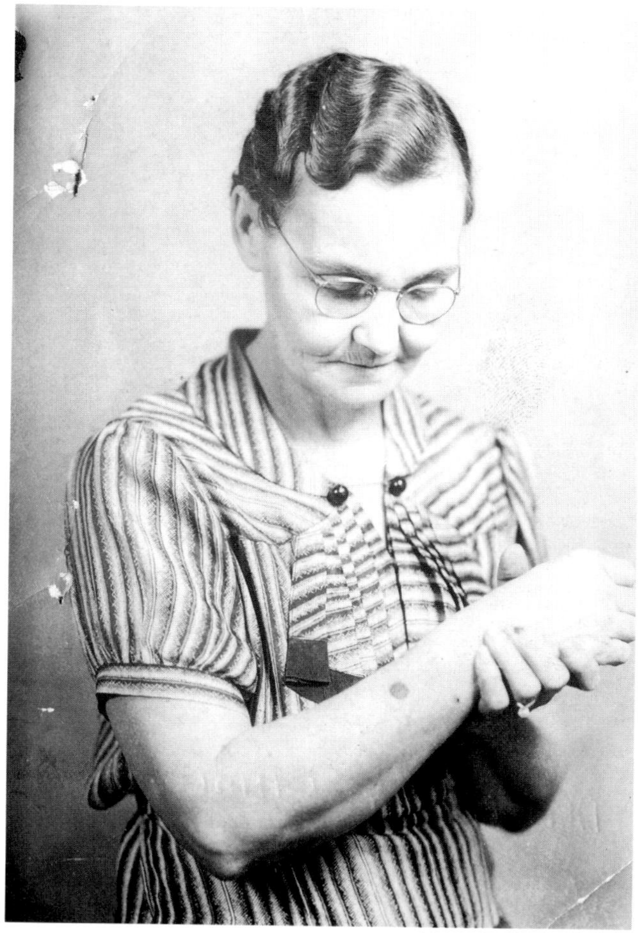

Suffering from an intense pain in her right arm, **MARION LINDLEY** of Springdale, ARKANSAS, went to a doctor who removed a steel needle an inch and a quarter in length from between the bones above her wrist. Mrs. Lindley eventually remembered that she had swallowed a needle when she was a young girl "running and looking up at some bluebirds." **The needle was in her body for thirty-six years. (February 11, 1935)**

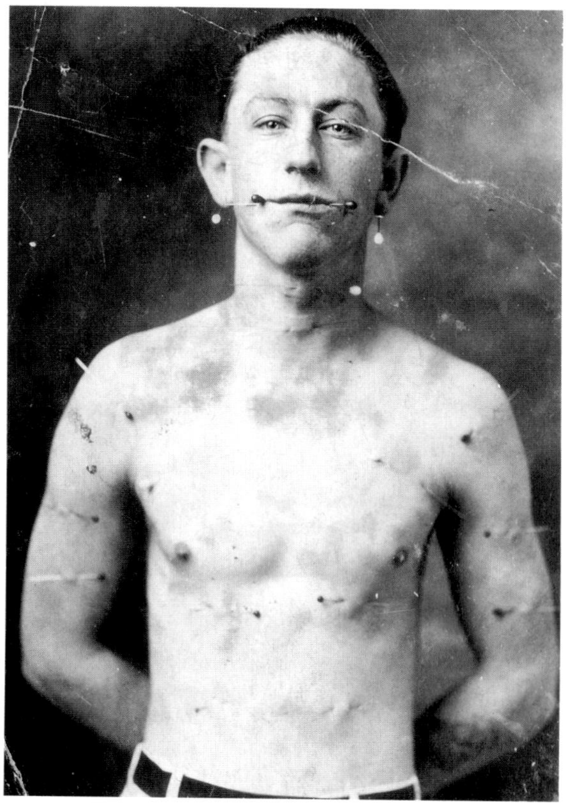

B. A. BRYANT of Waco, TEXAS, could stick as many as a **hundred pins and needles in his body at the same time.** This human pincushion claimed that he felt no pain while doing this. Mr. Bryant performed at the Dallas Odditorium in 1937 to the amazement of thousands. **(May 26, 1937)**

We have all heard that needles have eyes, but **El Gran Lazaro,** El Indio de Baracoa of Havana, could **put a needle in his eye socket and pull it out of his mouth! (February 21, 1935)**

FACE FACTS

"God has given you one face,
and you make yourselves another."

WILLIAM SHAKESPEARE

JIMMY DURANTE'S celebrated **schnozzola was insured for $100,000 by Lloyd's of London,** at considerably less than face value. **(November 4, 1932)**

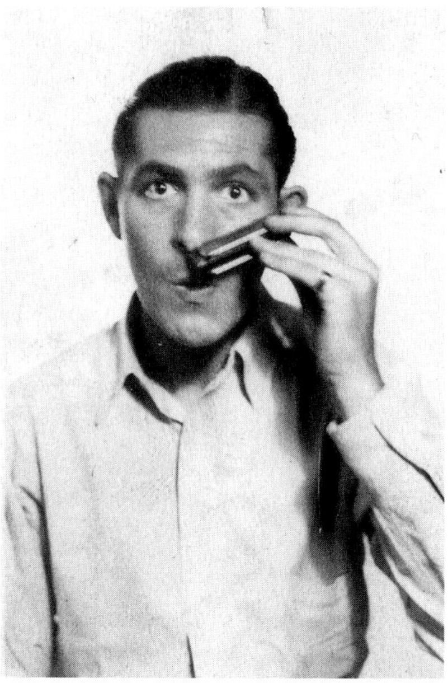

JACKIE GROSS of BOSTON could **whistle harmony while playing harmonica with his nose. (August 16, 1947)**

H. C. HARRIS, SR., played harmonica with his nose while whistling, in Jackson, MISSISSIPPI. All of the dozens of Ripley contestants who submitted their simultaneous whistling and harmonica-playing talents believed theirs was a unique skill. **(March 11, 1933)**

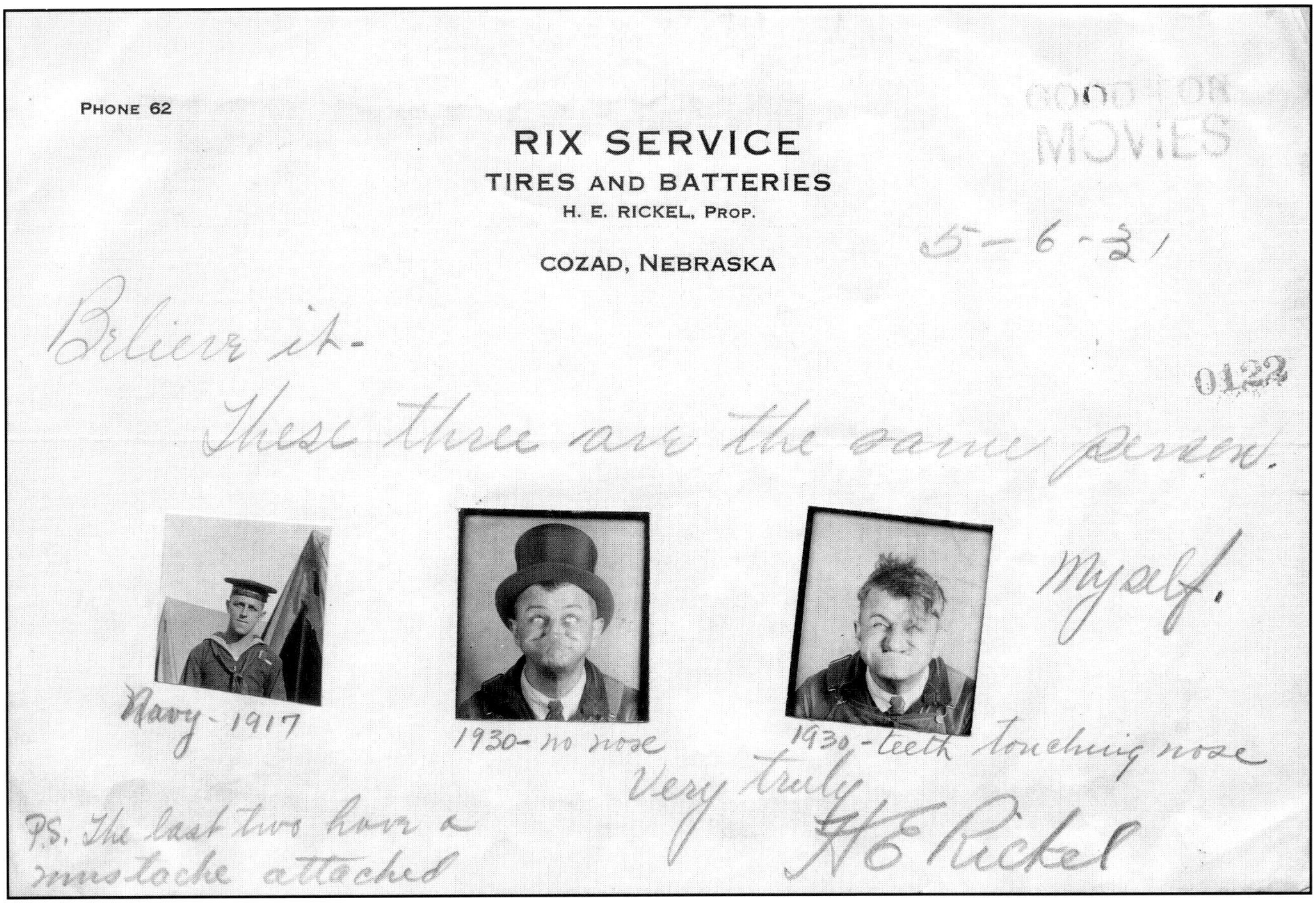

PHONE 62

RIX SERVICE
TIRES AND BATTERIES
H. E. RICKEL, PROP.

COZAD, NEBRASKA

GOOD FOR MOVIES

5-6-31

0122

Believe it-
These three are the same person.

Navy-1917

1930- no nose

1930-teeth touching nose

Myself.

Very truly
H E Rickel

P.S. The last two have a mustache attached

H. E. RICKEL could **touch his nose with his teeth,** in Cozad, NEBRASKA. **(November 1, 1931)**

J. T. SAYLORS of Villa Rica, GEORGIA, **had a face that could launch a thousand ships. (September 8, 1933)**

CLAUDE R. OVERHOLT of Marietta, OHIO, claimed he **could make over a hundred different faces.** He was declared a champion "ACROBATIC FACEMAKER" in New York City by those in the know. **(May 7, 1931)**

JAMES AAGAARD of Ord, NEBRASKA, **had a voice that could be heard over a distance of six miles.** He traveled the Midwest and Canada in the early 1930s presenting his "physical voice culture" theories and singing popular opera numbers. Arriving for one such performance at Plaster Rock, New Brunswick, in 1931, he discovered that there had been a mix-up in the advance publicity, and no one knew of the concert. Aagaard stepped outside the hall and sang two incredibly loud tenor solos, and within an hour people from throughout the county were lined up to attend the show! Aagaard was also said to be the best game shot in Nebraska. **(October 1, 1932)**

BOB RYAN, owner of the Park Restaurant in Hudson, NEW YORK, had **his front teeth replaced with seven gold ones set with a diamond in each.** After his restaurant folded he depended on welfare relief for support, refusing to disturb his teeth to retrieve the money they cost. **(June 20, 1938)**

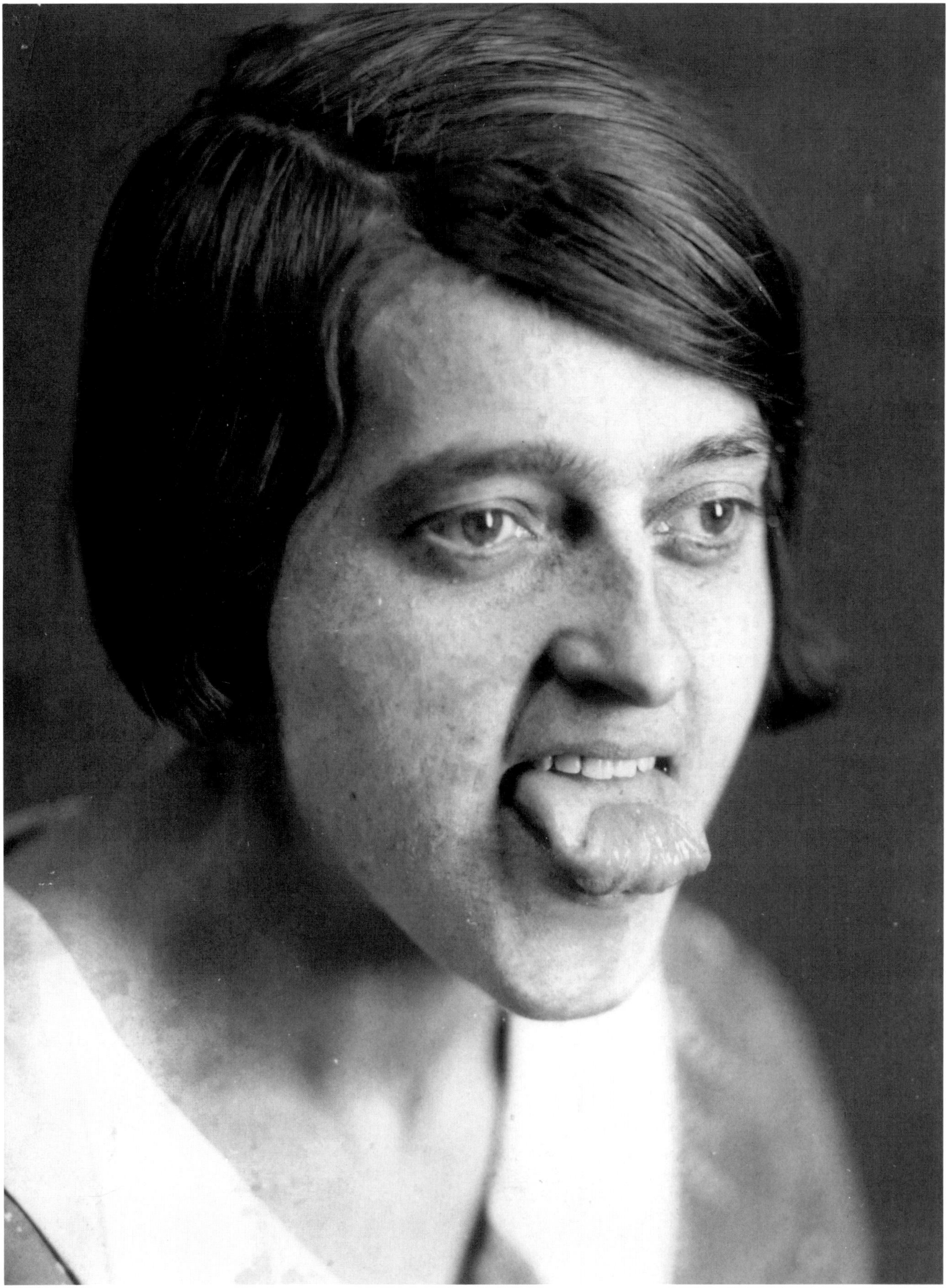

CHICAGO'S **SAUL BROWN blew saliva bubbles with smoke inside.** When they landed they popped like smoke bombs. **(May 30, 1935)**

Tongue-lapper **MARGUERITE ROSSELL** of Burlington, NEW JERSEY, **could fold her tongue at will. (May 6, 1933)**

'Most Sixty Years Ago Bullet Entered Eye; Coughed It Up Today

1921

West Point, Ga., March 21.—(Special.)—After carrying in his head for fifty-eight years, a bullet with which he was wounded in the eye at the battle of Vicksburg, July 1, 1863, W. V. Meadows today coughed up the bullet at his home here, and is feeling all right. Mr. Meadows, who was a member of G company, 37th Alabama infantry, was blinded in one eye by the bullet which he coughed up today.

W. V. MEADOWS of West Point, GEORGIA, was shot in the eye at the battle of Vicksburg on July 1, 1863. **Fifty-eight years later he unexpectedly coughed up the Civil War slug** (shown). **(July 21, 1932)**

Eastman Smiley of Hartford, Connecticut, had **a mustache twenty-five inches long. (October 10, 1948)**

Shown here is **Bertha Howard** of Prairie City, Oregon, who **could stand straight up on her five-foot-five-inch-long hair. (September 25, 1946)**

82

MRS. E. E. SMITH of Dallas, TEXAS, **grew her own hat.** Her Easter bonnet was crocheted out of the hair from her own head, which she had saved for eight years. A spiritualist, Mrs. Smith never allowed her hair to be cut and trusted in a regimen of facial calisthenics rather than allow herself the use of cosmetics. **(May 26, 1938)**

One-hundred-thirty-five-pound "LITTLE GIANT" **EDDIE POLO pulled a car with his hair** in Dover, NEW HAMPSHIRE. Later that evening he broke heavy chains with his chest, bent steel bars and horseshoes, and successfully challenged eight men to pull together against him in a tug of war. **(October 4, 1937)**

LEONA YOUNG, of Norwich, NEW YORK, **applies a blowtorch to her tongue.** A colleague of Professor Kongee, The Painless Wonder, Young called herself THE DEVIL'S DAUGHTER and **performed with hot lead, volcanic explosions,** and a regulation plumber's torch, which she **passed over her exposed flesh. (March 3, 1938)**

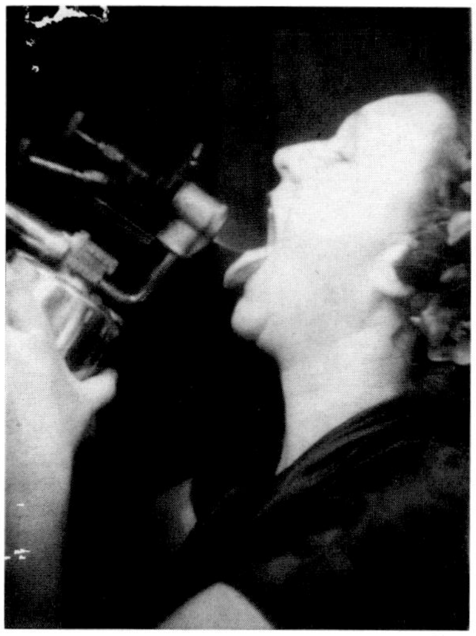

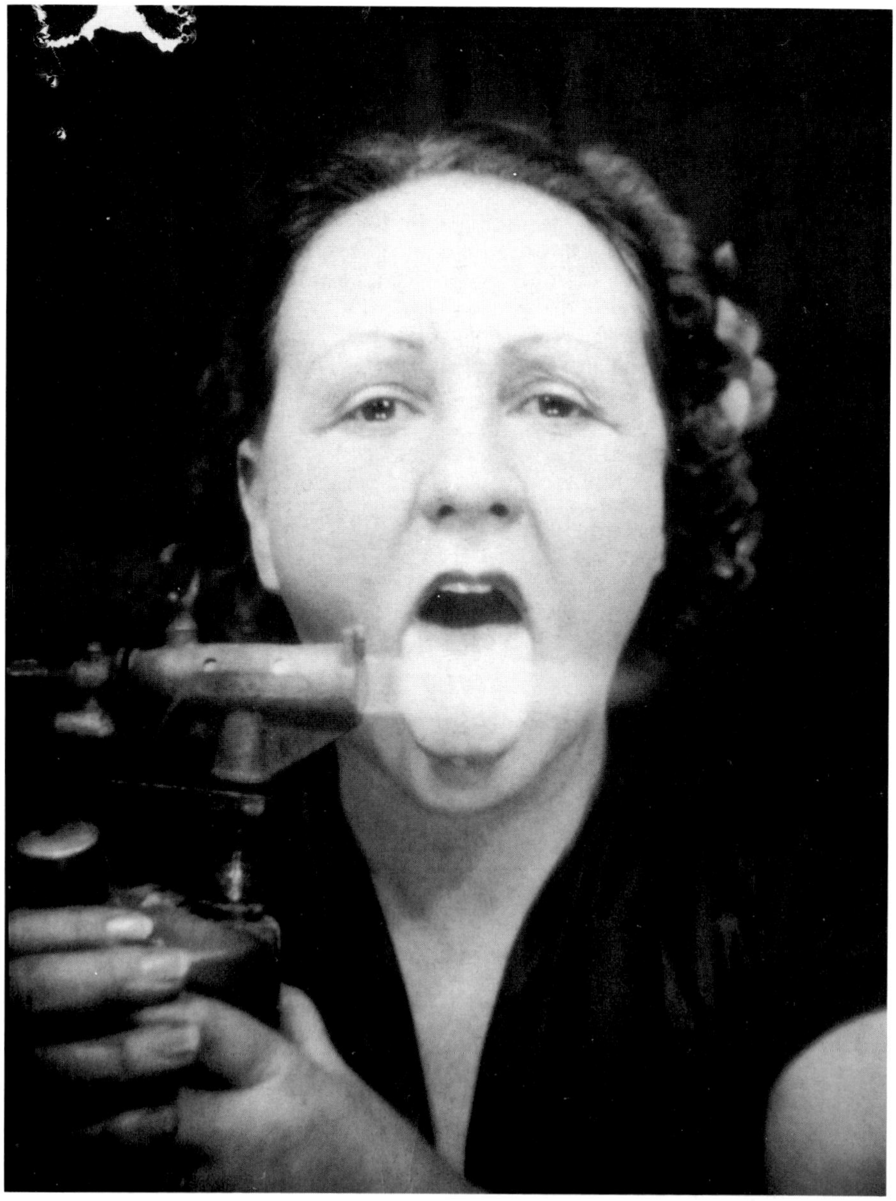

Theodore Kaufman licks a hot soldering iron in Astoria, Long Island. He could also pour molten lead into his cupped palm, after washing his hands with soap and water for fifteen minutes. **(June 26, 1953)**

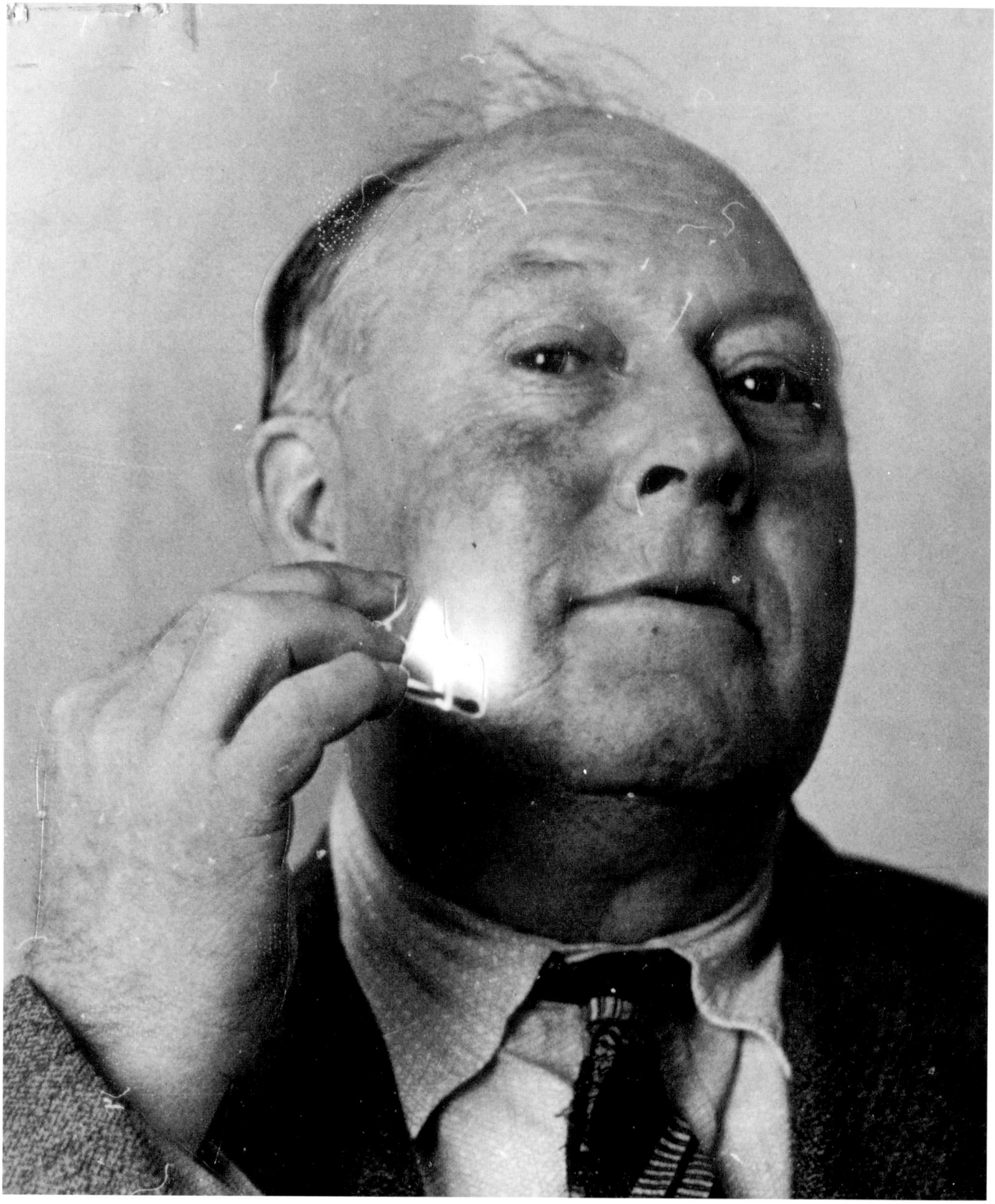

Edmonton, ALBERTA, boasted a citizen with "ASBESTOS SKIN." It seems a **MR. H. H. GETTY** walked into the editorial offices of the *Edmonton Bulletin* and proceeded to prove his fire-resisting abilities to a bug-eyed staff. Mr. Getty could **hold a lighted match close to the skin on various parts of his body** without any blistering or pain. **(May 20, 1940)**

Back at the beach just six weeks after giving birth, **ALICE RENO** of Allerton, MASSACHUSETTS, noticed that **a perfect portrait of her newborn had appeared on both her knees. (June 4, 1940)**

MARY SALZANO of North Bergen, NEW JERSEY, had a perfect **Cupid's face on her right knee. (February 14, 1950)**

Hold Everything

88

"An idea that is not dangerous is unworthy of being called an idea at all."

Oscar Wilde

Here is a man who could do many things well, and simultaneously! James J. Weir of Weirton, West Virginia, could hold a half-dollar in his eye, a pencil between his upper lip and nose, another pencil between his lower lip and chin, and a cigar between his teeth all while moving his scalp back and forth and singing. He claimed he had crossed the country twenty-nine times and asked upwards of 30,000 people to match his trick, but no one succeeded in duplicating the performance. **(June 18, 1932)**

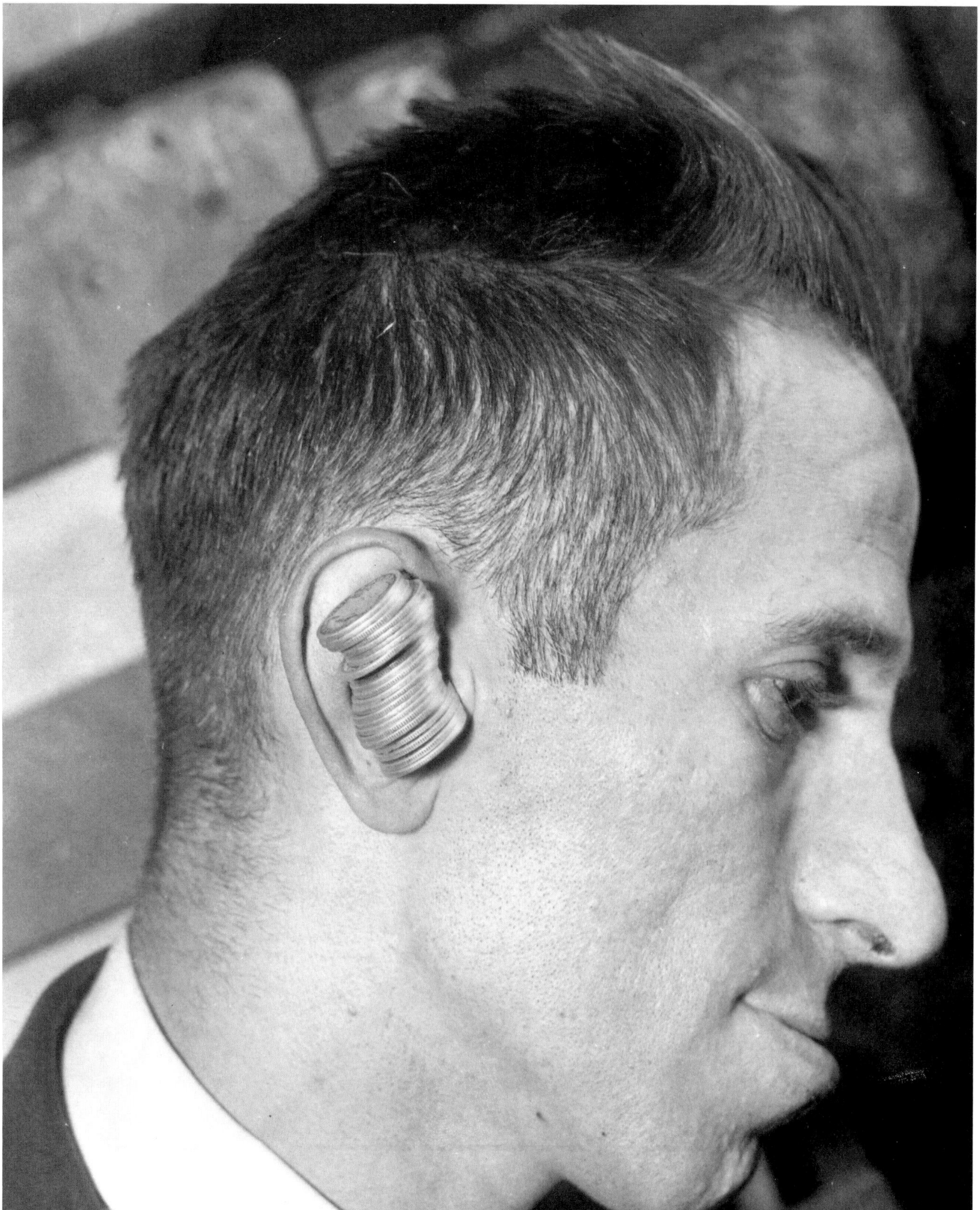

BROOKLYN'S **MAX CALVIN** never needed to fish for change. He could **hold twenty-five quarters in his ear! (July 15, 1933)**

Mt. Elliot Recreation employee **Bill Wausman** of Detroit insisted on **carrying a pencil** under, instead of above, his ear. Lobe and behold! **(February 2, 1942)**

Henry Gibbs lifts a whiskey bottle with his shoulder blades in Old Fort, North Carolina. This stunt won him third prize in an Asheville, North Carolina, Believe It or Not! contest. **(October 28, 1931)**

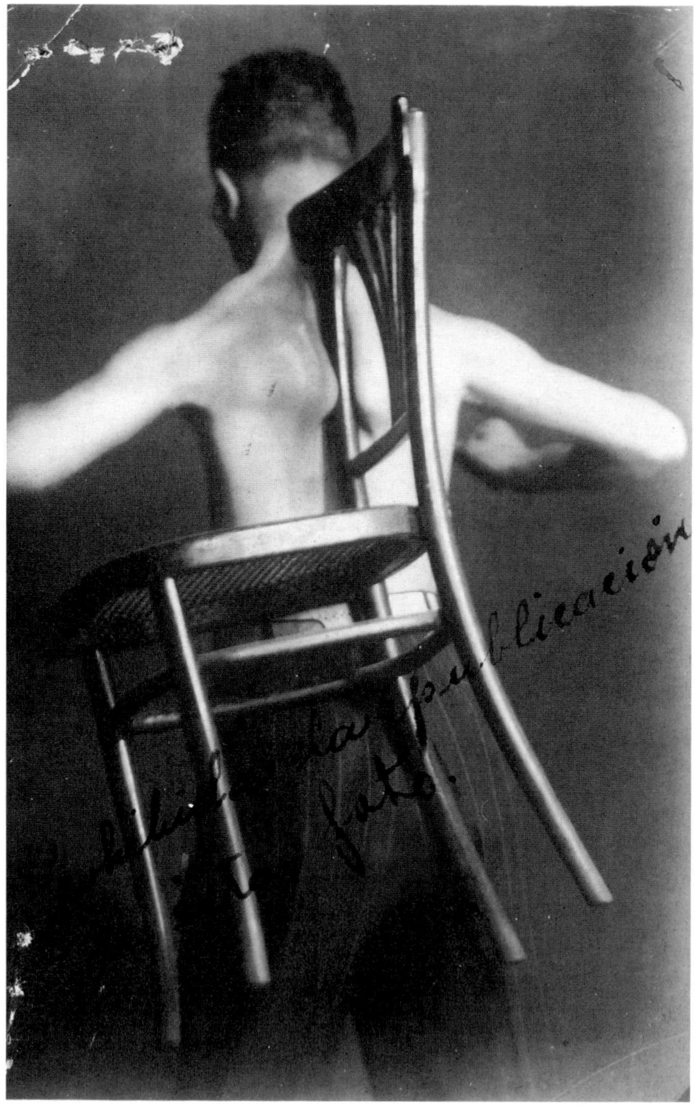

Feria Mundial lifts a chair with his shoulder blades in Mexico City. **(September 4, 1947)**

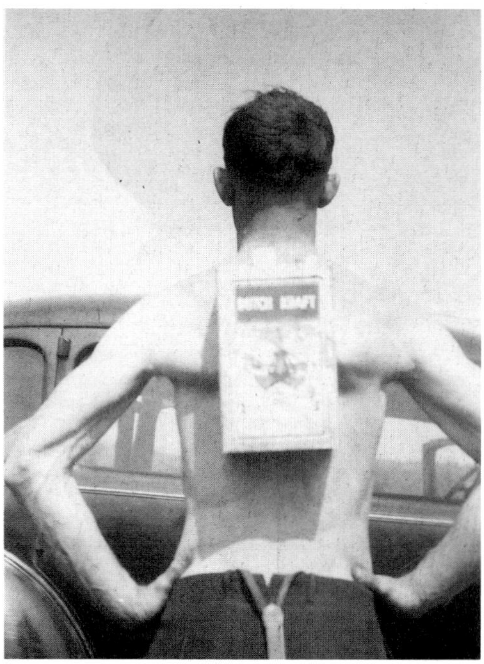

Grand Rapids native son **Joe Jirgles** could **hold a one-gallon varnish can between his shoulder blades.** He claimed he could attach himself to a fence this way so firmly that he could hang in place. **(March 14, 1945)**

Tomboy strong-girl **PATRICIA O'KEEFE—age eight—shown lifting 200-pound** Wayne Long in Santa Monica, CALIFORNIA. Patricia's weight: 64 pounds. Some weakling! **(March 6, 1940)**

Eleven-month-old **JUDITH ELAYNE ENTINE** of Philadelphia, PENNSYLVANIA, **performing a one-foot feat. (September 17, 1947)**

City team championship player **Alice Humbarger palms two basketballs** in Houston, Texas. The six-foot-four-inch jewelry salesperson could also reach two octaves on a piano with one hand, but she could not carry a tune. Item submitted by Miss Frances Short. **(September 6, 1931)**

Triple view of Master Engineer Junior Grade **Gardner A. Taylor lifting a 155-pound anvil with his ears,** at the Pheasant Hunters Banquet in Winner, South Dakota. Later the sixty-four-year-old war veteran broke his own record by adding a 20-pound weight to the same anvil at the Peacock Café. Sixteen years later he was still going strong, lifting a 110-pound anvil with his ears on his eightieth birthday. **(March 10, 1944)**

MENTAL MARVELS, WIZARDS, AND PRODIGIES

"What you don't know would make a great book."

SYDNEY SMITH

MR. GEORGE BOVE of the BRONX demonstrated a unique and curious ability in the Believe It or Not! office in 1933. **By suspending a key on a silk thread and dangling it over a specimen of handwriting he was able to tell the sex of the person who wrote it.** The staff at Ripley's gave him dozens of examples, and he never failed to come up with the correct response. Baffled by this demonstration, Ripley sent a query over to Bellevue Hospital in NEW YORK to see if anyone there could shed any light on the phenomenon. A Dr. Brooke seemed to think this might be the first true case of **"sexographia"** on record. Bove maintained that he could sense the electricity of people through their handwriting, and that men have a different "wattage" than women. Simple. **(September 25, 1933)**

OSCAR SPURGEON of Salem, INDIANA, could **read newspapers and books upside down** or at any other angle. **(December 31, 1935)**

MISS CECIL EDNA KING of LOS ANGELES could **read a book just as fast holding it upside down** as right side up. **(November 3, 1941)**

C. J. ANDERSON of Spring City, UTAH, **wrote all correspondence upside down and backwards. (July 11, 1938)**

Miss Zelma George of Canton, Ohio, **could write forwards, backwards, upside down, and upside down backwards,** and also write a different sentence with each hand in any combination of upside down, backwards, etc., simultaneously. Whew! **(January 5, 1948)**

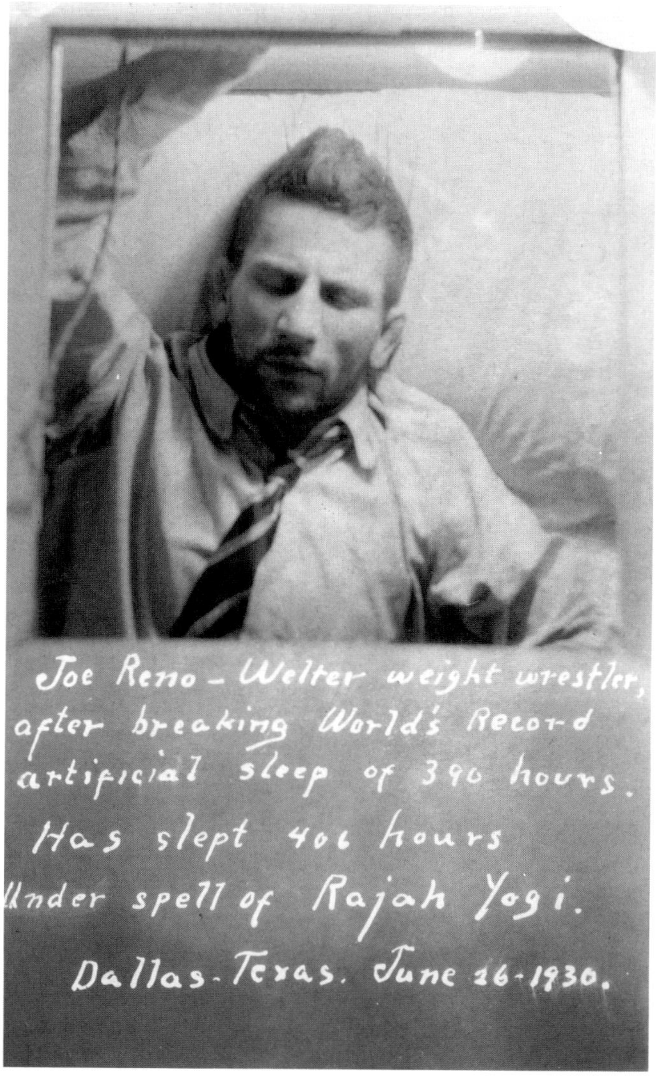

U.S. Navy wrestling champion **Joe Reno,** hypnotized by **Rajah Yogi** in Dallas, Texas, **slept buried in a coffin for nearly seventeen days in June 1930 without food or water** to set a new world record for hypnotic sleep. Within fifteen minutes after being reawakened by Rajah Yogi, Reno wrestled Shreveport, Louisiana, middleweight champion Red Lindsay to a ten-minute draw! **(February 3, 1931)**

Eastern mystic and hypnotic trance man **Rajah Yogi** of Oklahoma autographed this promotional photograph for presentation to Ripley **after waking Joe Reno from his record-breaking slumber. (December 11, 1934)**

Beleive it or not, to Mr Robert L. Ripley;
with my admiration and gratitude.
Rajah Yogi.
March 22-1933.

NATURE'S WHIMS

102

"There is nothing so powerful as
truth–and often nothing so strange."

DANIEL WEBSTER

MISS MARIE IDAH BRUNOZZY of Wanamie, PENNSYLVANIA, **spent three years and eight months growing these attractive fingernails** —the longest of which was 5 3/8 inches. Employed in a children's toy store, she claimed the children admired her nails and would stop in the shop just to see how things were growing. **(June 29, 1953)**

An unknown patient at the Soochow Hospital in CHINA here displays his world-record fingernails. He had a **thirty-three-inch fingernail that took forty-four years to grow,** and his "little" fingernail was fifteen inches long. **(January 15, 1935)**

WENG, THE HUMAN UNICORN, a Chinese farmer **with a thirteen-inch horn growing out of his head,** briefly exhibited himself in the early 1930s among a company of Chinese fakirs in Fuchiatien, MANCHURIA, where this snapshot was taken by a Russian employee of the National City Bank of New York. For years Ripley offered large rewards to anyone who could find him again and bring him to America for an Odditorium appearance. **(May 11, 1930)**

This horned rooster was the Pride of the White Owl Café, owned by **JESSE T. PARKER** of DeQueen, ARKANSAS. **(December 23, 1931)**

FRANCESCO LENTINI of SICILY **was born with three legs.** He used two legs for walking and the third as a chair to sit on. He was for many years a part of Buffalo Bill's Wild West Show and an ace soccer player.

WILLIAM H. RAINEY of Fort Worth, TEXAS, holds his **four-foot-eleven-inch Snake Cucumber. (April 14, 1930)**

A. B. TYLER found an edible **21-pound 14-ounce giant puffball fungus** near his home in Cattaraugus County, NEW YORK. It briefly held the record for the biggest reported in a season of unusually large puffballs, broken only a few weeks later when B. H. Kippenstein brought a 28-pound 8-ounce monster to the Manitou, Manitoba, post office for a weigh-in. Puffballs are near cousins to mushrooms. **(October 24, 1931)**

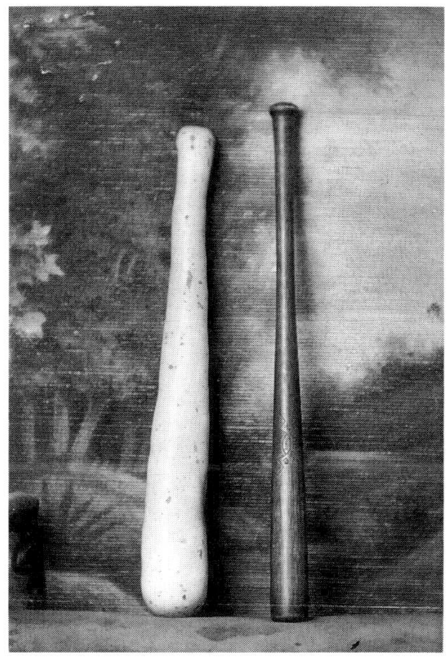

A gourd in the shape of a baseball bat was grown near Ft. Worth, TEXAS, by **MILLER DANIEL** on the Glenn Brothers Ranch. This variety, sometimes called a dishrag gourd, rarely grows to the whopping dimensions of this 32-inch slugger. **(November 20, 1945)**

Carrot hand found by **Tommy Andrews** at the Palace Café, Redlands, California. **(May 11, 1935)**

Carrot hand grown by **M. L. Little** of Bellingham, Washington. **(January 10, 1932)**

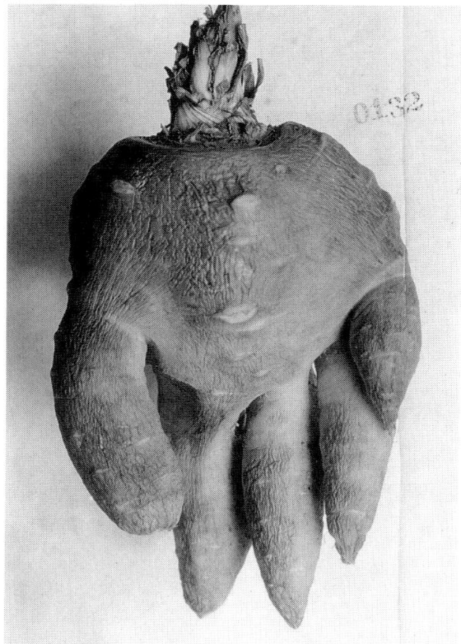

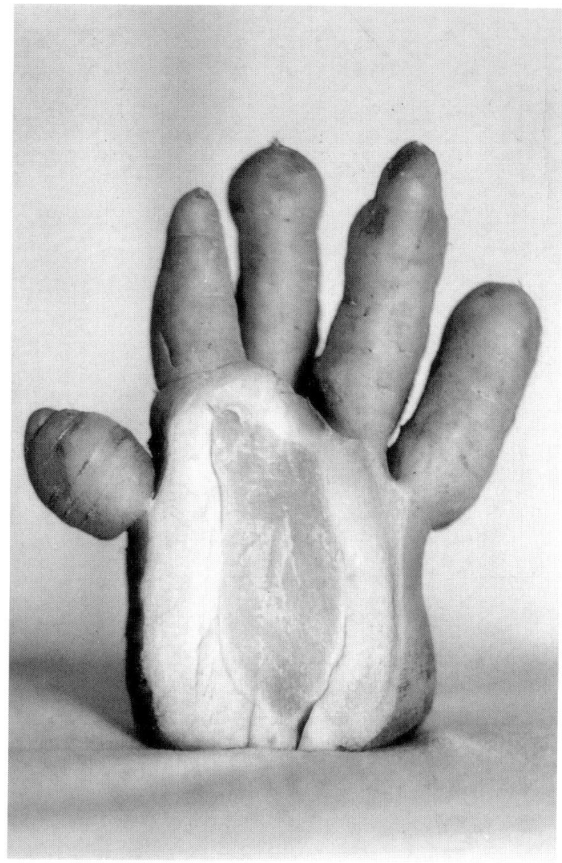

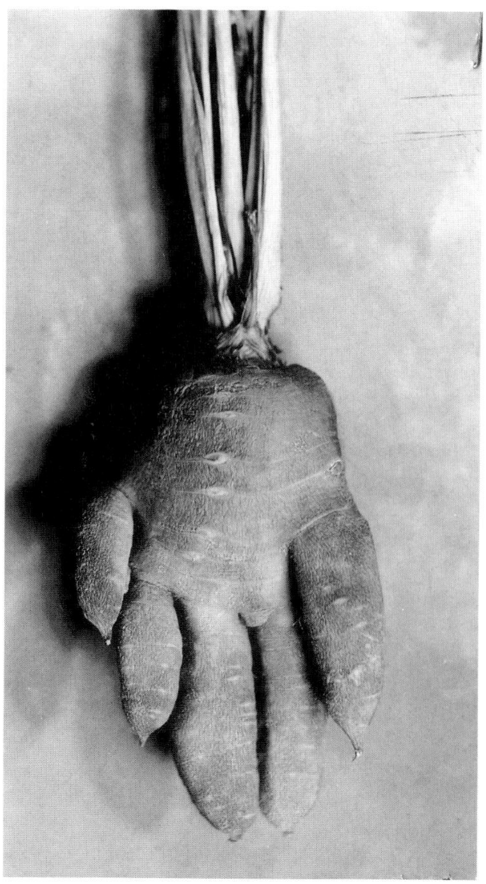

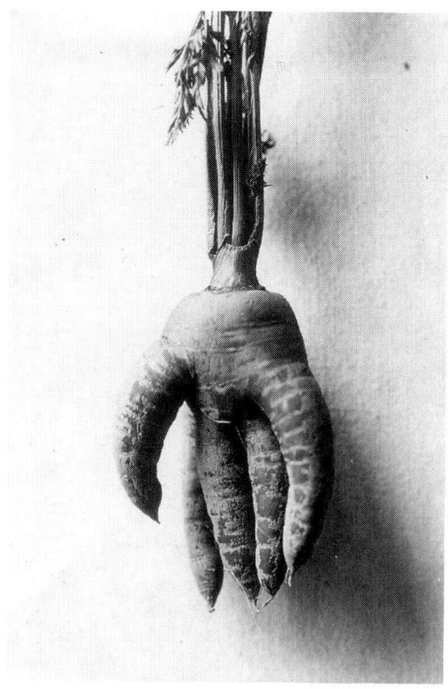

Carrot hand grown by **Alexander Moe** of Brainerd, Minnesota. **(December 12, 1932)**

Carrot hand grown by **Harry Sims**, Grand Prairie, Alberta, Canada. **(November 5, 1940)**

Singing and playing piano were just two of the extraordinary talents of toy shepherd **LADY TRILLING** of Hollywood, CALIFORNIA. Her trainer, **MRS. ADELA FOWLER,** could not play a note. **(November 23, 1947)**

A nearsighted rock cod was caught sporting spectacles in the waters off Bellingham, WASHINGTON. As if that were not enough, the glasses were identified by **IRA D. ERLING,** salesman, as his own. It seems his glasses went overboard while he was out trolling for salmon in the same area where the fish was caught. **(April 9, 1940)**

This vaudeville roller-skating dog was owned and trained by **FRANK JACOBS** of New Castle, MAINE. Although Jacobs occasionally presented the dog in local theater performances, his Riverview Restaurant business kept him too busy to make a career out of his sensational skating canine. **(August 4, 1931)**

TEX, part bulldog and part bird dog, was only 22 inches tall but 44 inches around and weighed 120 pounds! His owner, **IRMA FAREK** of Hockley, TEXAS, says his favorite food was lemon snaps, which he is holding in the picture. **(August 22, 1932)**

The Wild Duck with the Human Mind was owned by **F. G. CLARK** of CHICAGO. Shown here out for a walk with Clark, it could distinguish between coins, and it is said to have displayed signs of patriotism. **(September 21, 1933)**

Craigsville, VIRGINIA, could boast **a horse with a perfect Indian head on it.** This horse was born on August 15, 1935, to owners **R. L. ANDERSON and J. F. DANIEL. (June 14, 1940)**

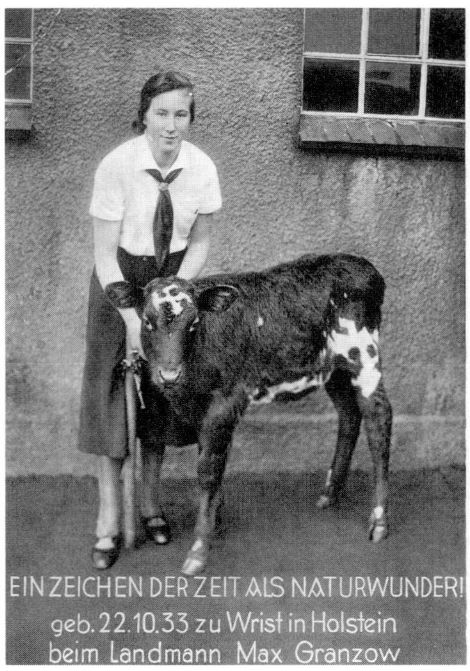

Up in Port Townsend, WASHINGTON, **trout were trained to jump through a hoop.** Item submitted by **W. R. RAMSEY. (July 10, 1931)**

Translation: A Sign of the Times—calf born October 22, 1933, at Wrist-Holstein, GERMANY, **with a Nazi cross on its forehead.** Farmer/owner **MAX GRANZOW** was stunned by this amazing coincidence. **(April 10, 1934)**

Cow with "7," born on July 7, 1937, on **CHRIS WATTENBERG'S** farm in Brighton, COLORADO. **(August 2, 1938)**

Calf with a perfect "7" on its head. Submitted by **CARL MARTINSEN** of Bellingham, WASHINGTON. **(December 5, 1955)**

Heifer with a perfect "7" on its head. Owned by **CLETUS BUECHNER** of Convoy, OHIO. **(July 15, 1952)**

Cow with "7," Croswell, MICHIGAN. Submitted by **BETTY VARRIALE. (December 5, 1936)**

This pup has a chicken on his hindquarters. His name and that of his owner are lost to history, but **MR. V. K. BIGALKE** of CHICAGO sent in this snap for Ripley's approval. **(February 9, 1931)**

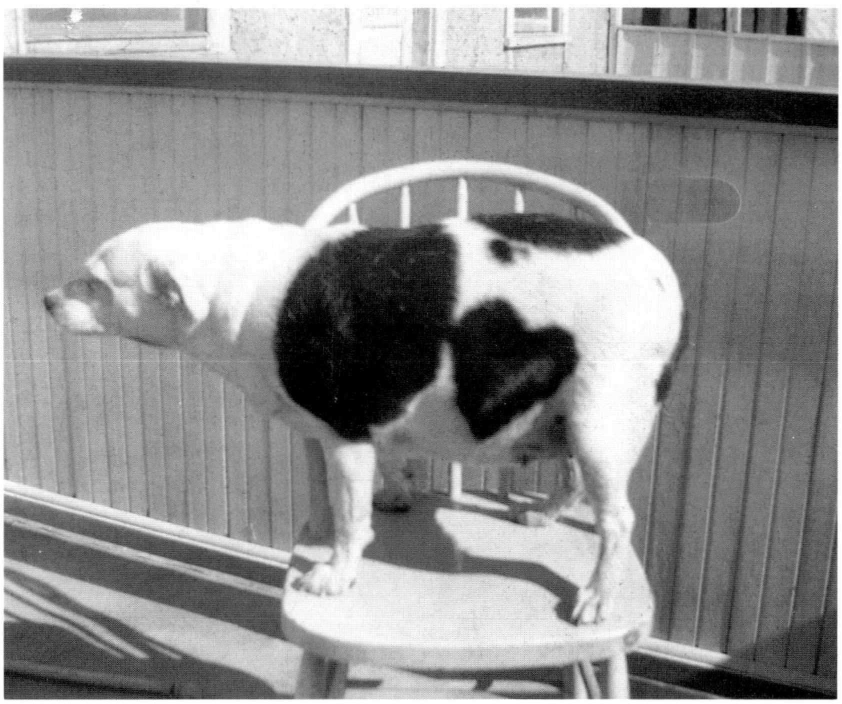

Patches, a dog with two hearts, owned by **JACK RIMOL** of Casa Grande, ARIZONA, was fond of mint-flavored chewing gum and wore cowboy outfits on special occasions. She earned an A-1 Credit Rating at the local Pioneer Meat Market. **(October 24, 1939)**

Sweetheart, **a horse with two hearts,** owned by **MRS. WEAVER BLAKE** of Humboldt, KANSAS, was blind and had prosthetic eyes made of glass. **(May 7, 1939)**

This **black bear with a white heart** lived near Beckley, WEST VIRGINIA. Submitted by **CHARLES DE SPAIN. (July 28, 1939)**

Ginger, a ten-month-old **fox terrier with two hearts,** was owned by **Edna Markham** of Hollywood, CALIFORNIA. **(May 30, 1936)**

Cow with a perfect heart, born on Valentine's Day. Submitted by **MRS. L. E. KIRBY** of Florence, SOUTH CAROLINA. **(February 14, 1952)**

This lamb **with a perfect heart on its shoulders,** (also) born on Valentine's Day, was owned by **LEE EPPERSON** of Edina, MISSOURI. **(May 6, 1938)**

Two sets of twins both named Loretta and Lorraine Szymanski attended the same school, were in the same classroom, and lived just a few doors apart on the same street in Pittsburgh, but were not related! Their teacher was the first to discover the amazing coincidence. **(July 20, 1955)**

After fifteen years of regularly being mistaken for another woman in the same city, Vivian Weiss finally met her double, Mrs. Joseph Pepper. Both, as it turned out, had the same birthday, the same wedding anniversary, the same stomach ailments, the same food likes and dislikes, and both had three children almost exactly the same ages. They met one night at a party in Omaha, Nebraska, after discovering that both had hurt their legs in the same way at the same place on the same day. **(July 2, 1939)**

Identical twins MAX and BERNARD FRIEDMAN bought identical coats without the knowledge of the other brother in stores 350 miles apart. Bernard lived in East Chicago, INDIANA, and Max lived in Des Moines, IOWA, but both purchased light plaid topcoats with the serial number 17343, only discovering the coincidence months later. **(March 28, 1943)**

Never/Always

"Most people would succeed in small things if they were not troubled with great ambitions."

Henry Wadsworth Longfellow

This brother-and-sister **duo had twenty-two years of perfect attendance between them.** At Alachua High School in Alachua, Florida, student **Eunice Cox** completed twelve years of schooling in ten years without being absent or tardy. When her baby brother was an infant, their mother whispered into young **John Cox, Jr.'s** ear that she hoped that he too might be 100 percent loyal to his school. Sure enough, he graduated from the same school without being absent or tardy for twelve years. Submitted by **H. L. Rockwood,** former principal of the school. **(October 25, 1936)**

Never-Never Man **SIMON P. CRONE** of Brunswick, MARYLAND, age seventy-five, **had never done many things.** Among the things he had never done: shot a gun, read a novel, used tobacco or liquor, been married or had a sweetheart, crossed a river, or been out of the county where he was born. He also used the same pencil for fifty years. The cost of the pencil was one penny. **(September 15, 1935)**

Can you top this? **At age thirty-six, Roy Robert Smith** of Denver, COLORADO, had never tasted an ice cream soda, Coca-Cola, ginger ale, wine, beer, or whiskey; never used tobacco in any form, never dipped snuff; **never gone swimming,** hunting, fishing, hiking, or ice-skating; never played football, billiards, poker, cards, baseball, basketball, tennis, golf, hockey, or polo; **never pitched a horseshoe;** never driven a car or ridden a bicycle, motorcycle, or horse; never seen an earthquake, flood, or tornado, nor **witnessed a fatal accident;** never seen a race of any kind; never been inside a saloon or speakeasy; never been struck or stunned by lightning or bitten by any kind of animal, reptile, or poisonous insect; never had a surgical operation; never shot a gun, pistol, rifle, or cannon; never been robbed or burglarized; never participated in a fight; never gambled nor bet; never been aboard a steamship or yacht; never ridden in a balloon or airplane; **never milked a cow or goat; never** been **underground in a cave** or mine; never joined a club, lodge, church, or organization; never seen a bullfight or duel; never harnessed a horse; never attended a rodeo; never been in a lumber camp, sawmill, granary, or foundry; never studied a foreign language; never been outside the United States; never been convicted of a crime; **never fainted;** never been inside a penitentiary, nor **been a patient in a hospital or sanatorium;** never kissed a girl; and never been engaged to marry. **(March 18, 1934)**

Dennis Cullen of Galesburg, ILLINOIS, **at seventy years of age had never tasted chicken.** What's more, Mr. Cullen had been a locomotive fireman for the C. B. and Q. Railroad for thirty years and claimed he had not had a drink of water in forty years. **(May 1, 1932)**

Ben Seiff, the Barber of Venice, California, **had a headache for twenty-six years** but never missed a day's work. Seiff lived on Ozone Street. **(September 22, 1932)**

Enoch Bailey, of Columbia, South Carolina, actually **shaved every morning for thirty years!** You could say he made it into immortality by a close shave. **(May 2, 1935)**

The fact that he was not a winner at fishing made **O. H. L. Bell** of Chillicothe, Texas, all the more appealing for a Ripley cartoon. It seems that Bell fished often and in areas where others fishing beside him were bringing in good fish, but he never managed to even get a nibble at his bait. **He fished for six years** with both live bait and artificial lures **without ever once feeling the quiver of a fish. (February 15, 1935)**

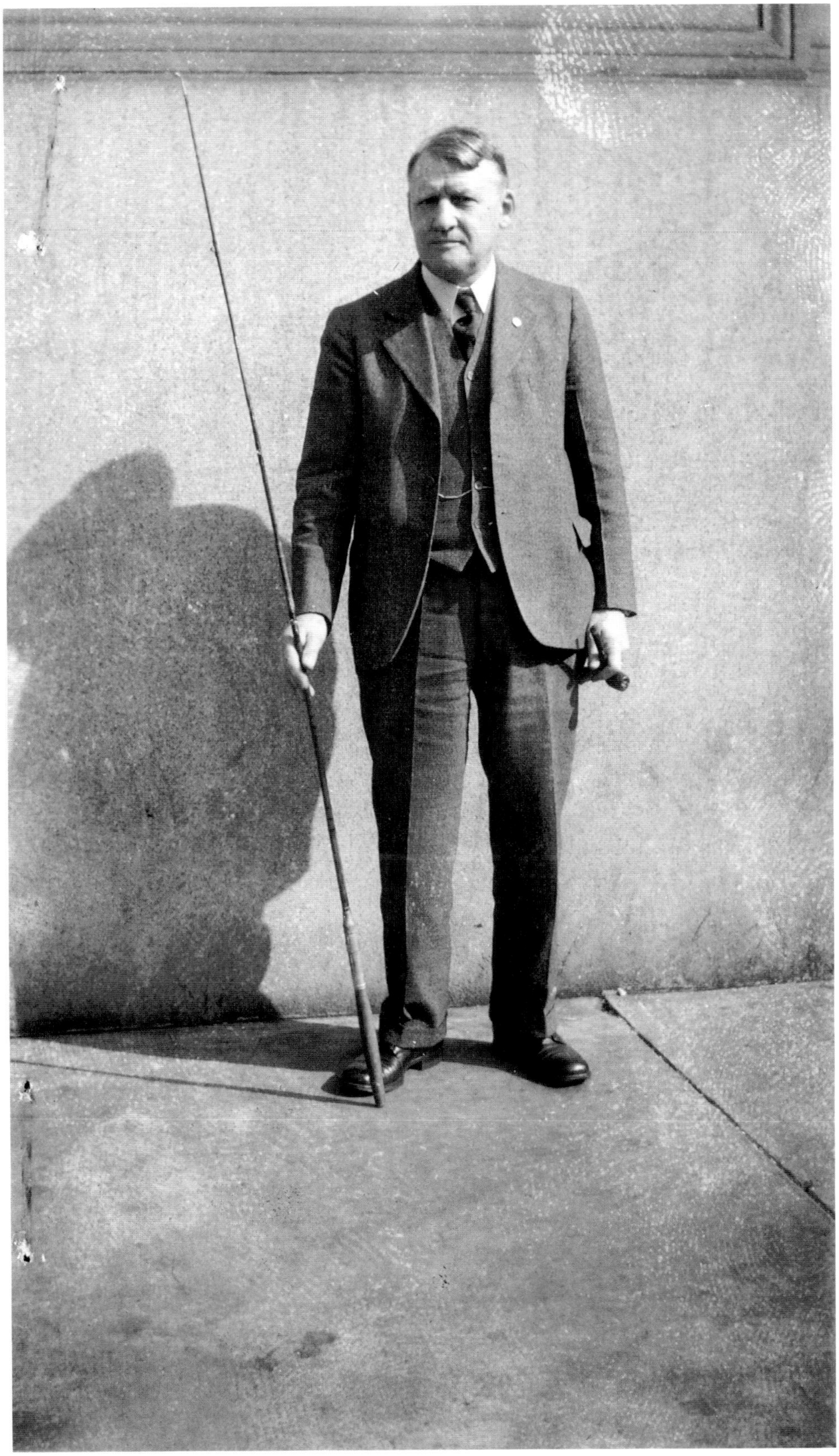

Audacious angler **F. D. HILL,** Treasurer of the Life Insurance Company of VIRGINIA, **caught 30,578 fish in forty years with the same rod.** Item submitted by M. M. Gregory. **(March 13, 1935)**

Where There's Smoke

130

"It is easier to suppress the first desire than to satisfy all that follow it."

Benjamin Franklin

Shown here is **two-year-old Leslie Louis Young,** of Nicholasville, Kentucky, **relaxed with his pipe** and tobacco after a tough afternoon playing in the sandbox. **(August 17, 1931)**

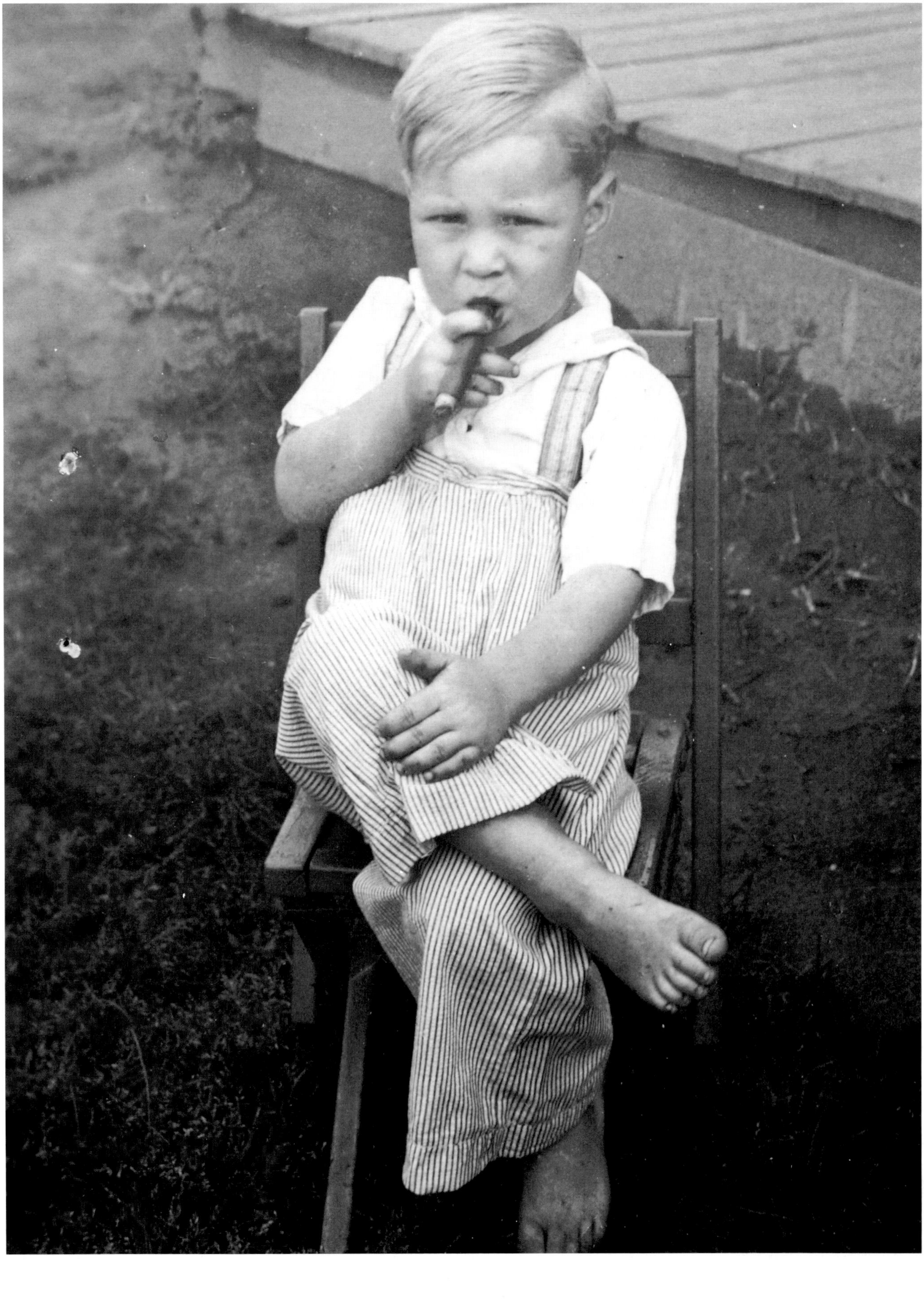

W. J. EVANS of Poteau, OKALAHOMA, **could hold a dime between his chin and nose,** while smoking. **(April 9, 1948)**

MRS. BELLE RYANS of Savannah, GEORGIA, **smoked a pipe every day for more than a hundred years,** but she didn't approve of young flappers smoking cigarettes. She far outlived her sons, who died fighting for the Confederacy, but never realized her ambition of flying in an airplane. She was 109 years old in this photograph and lived to the ripe old age of 119! **(March 10, 1931)**

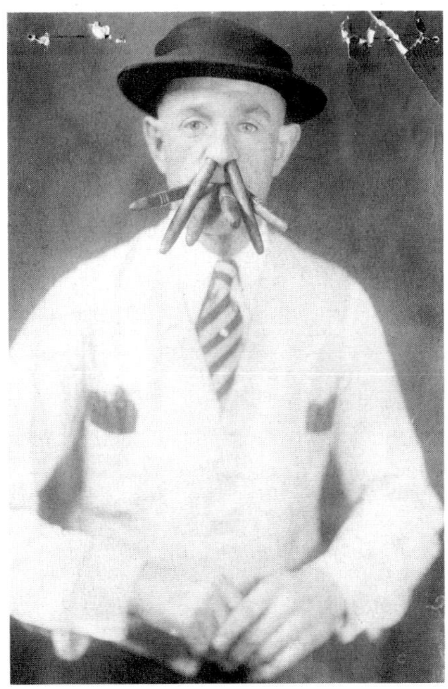

By the time **he was three, JOHN MULLICAN, JR., had been smoking for more than two years.** The McAlester, OKLAHOMA, youngster started with a pipe but soon switched to smoking two White Owl cigars a day and the occasional store-bought cigarette. He didn't care much for candy and refused to chew anything but Brown Mule Tobacco in between smokes. When this picture was taken, Johnny was described as "healthy in every way," seldom suffering from nervous attack or common colds despite the fact that he insisted "on going 'round with very little clothes even in the winter time." **(July 18, 1935)**

JOHNNY "CIGAR" CONNORS of Roxbury, MASSACHUSETTS, held the record for **smoking 600 cigars in forty-eight hours** without eating, drinking, or sleeping. **(February 25, 1933)**

The only dog
in the world
who actually
smokes!
The dog has no
hat on!
=Hello=
Good-friend=
Bill Sharples
& Artur
Paramount K.
Hollywood

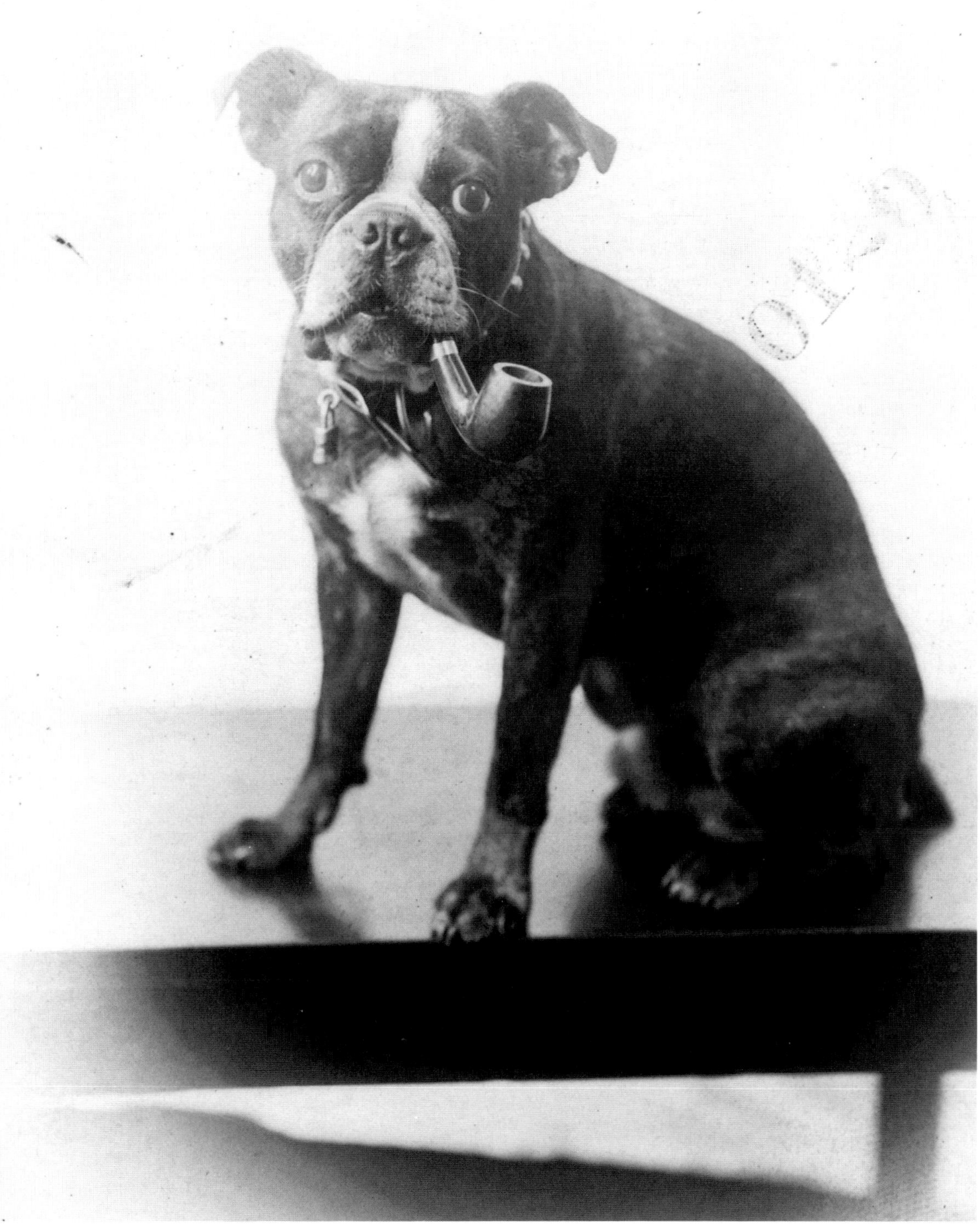

George Kohan, of Smithers, West Virginia, had a three-year-old dog named Briddle, who **not only smoked a pipe and cigarettes but could tell the time of day,** day of the week, date of the month, and perform all four functions of arithmetic. **(October 24, 1931)**

Here's **Bill Sharples** with Artur, **the only dog in the world who took up the smoking habit,** in Hollywood. **(February 14, 1932)**

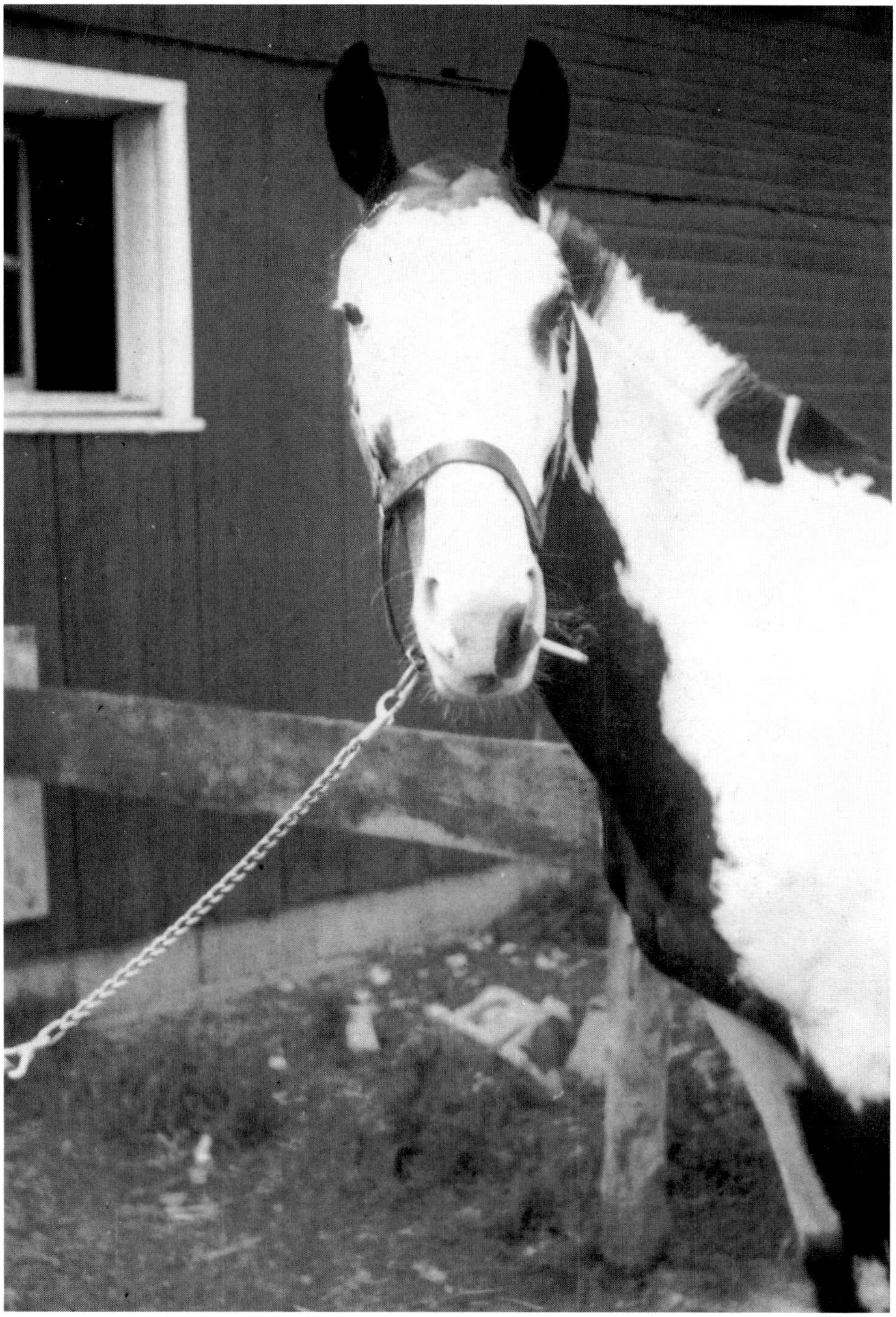

Out behind the stables **HANS STEINMETZ** of Durand, MICHIGAN, **taught his horse to smoke and inhale cigarettes. (November 2, 1950)**

A white Australorp rooster belonging to the Woodside Poultry Farm of Neenah, WISCONSIN, **gazed contentedly at his prize ribbons while enjoying a smoke. (May 28, 1934)**

Suspended Animation

"No knowledge can be more satisfactory to a man than that of his own frame, its parts, their functions and actions."

Thomas Jefferson

Milkman **Henry O. Darken** and his seven-year-old daughter, **Nancy Joyce Darken,** tripped the light fantastic as an **upside-down trumpet-playing and tap-dancing duo.** They performed their novelty act in the Chicago suburb of Elmwood Park, Illinois. **(October 9, 1938)**

Theatrical
CHICAGO

Cornish immigrant **UNCLE BILLY HOOPER,** shown in front of his farmhouse in Lebanon, KANSAS, **could still stand on his head at the age of eighty-six. (March 12, 1935)**

SALT LAKE CITY letter carrier **FRANK OLSEN** did the **can-can on his hands while playing his own accompaniment on the harmonica. (May 2, 1935)**

55

BROOKLYN strong man **RAYMOND VAN CLEEF could lift a 110-pound anvil with his teeth while doing a handstand.** Van Cleef's stationery proclaims his membership in the New York Society of Graduate Medical Gymnasts & Masseurs. **(March 25, 1934)**

SIEGMUND KLEIN could do five sets of ten dips or vertical pushups (fifty in all) without having to pause for a rest. Due to his mastery of unusual physical abilities, Ripley frequently consulted with Klein on items submitted that required specialized knowledge of the capabilities of the human body. **(November 8, 1941)**

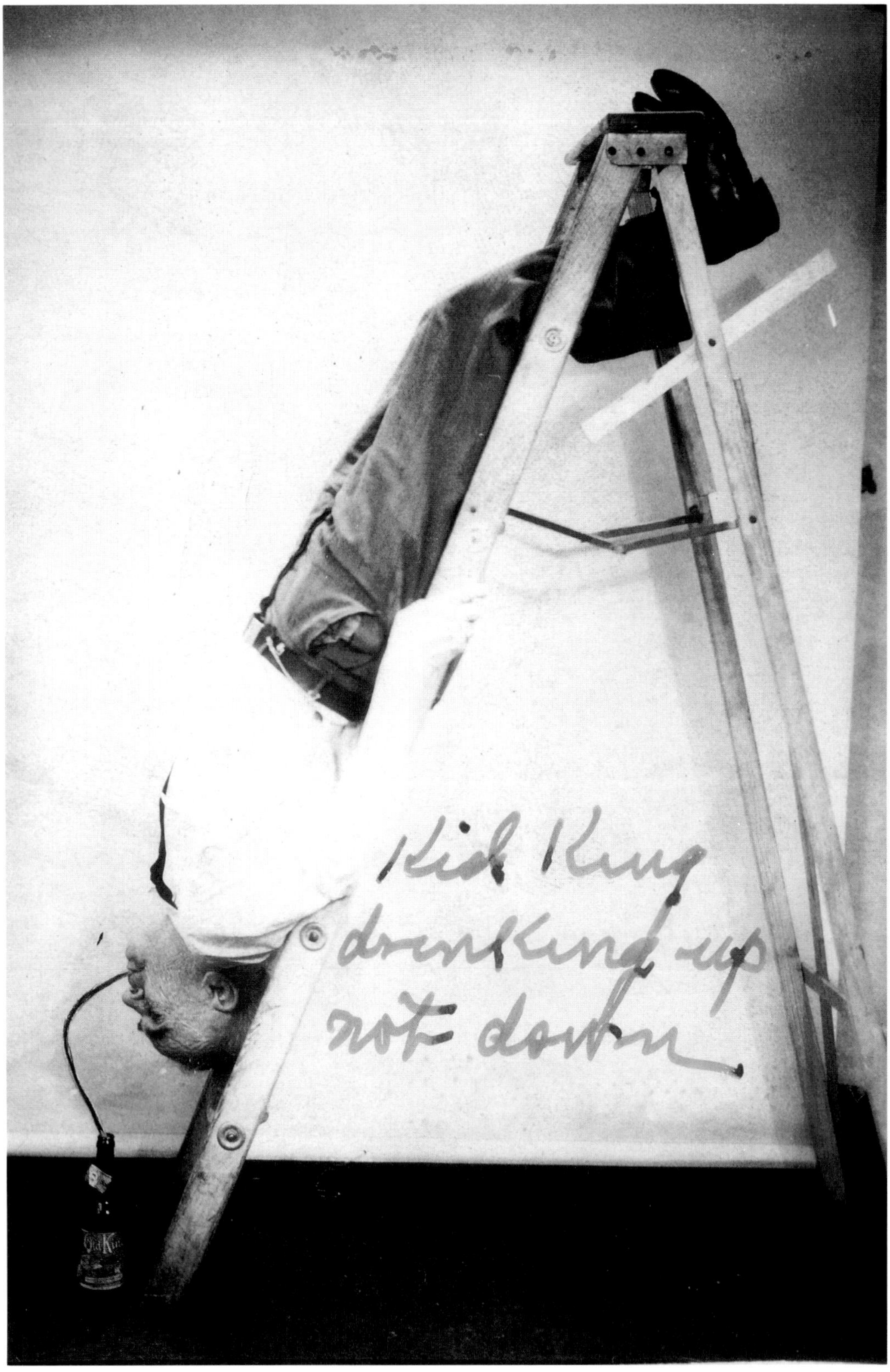

OKLAHOMA CITY foot racer **F. W. S. "KID" KING** saw two mules leaning down a steep embankment to quench their thirsts at a waterfall and **concocted the idea of teaching himself to drink upside down.** He perfected the skill after a few practice tries and won $25 in a DENVER bar a few years later by betting another man that he could drink a bottle of beer without a drop going down his throat. Twenty-six years later (at age seventy-three) he repeated the stunt for Ripley. **(January 7, 1937)**

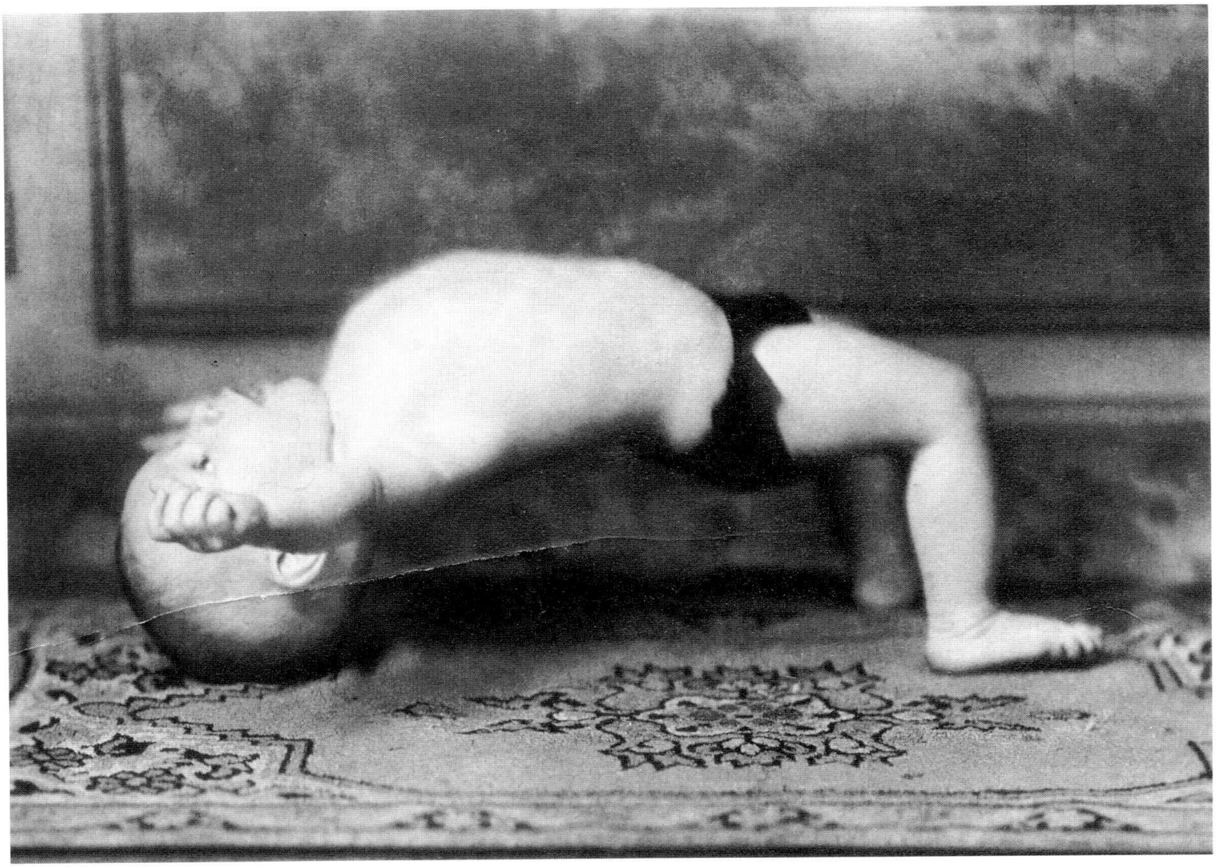

Ralph Roland Dowell did his first **perfect "wrestler's bridge"** in Grand Junction, Colorado, **at the age of two and a half months.** By the time he was six months old he could hold the position for more than two minutes. **(January 9, 1932)**

Ted Elbert Carmack, at three and a half months old, could lift his own weight on a chin-up bar. His father, an Army officer stationed in Denver, began young Ted's physical conditioning when the boy was three weeks old. **(December 19, 1934)**

At seventy-four years of age, MRS. F. M. IRWIN of Raleigh, NORTH CAROLINA, could still do more work than the average woman of twenty, **run as fast as the average girl of sixteen,** and still do chin-ups. **(June 9, 1940)**

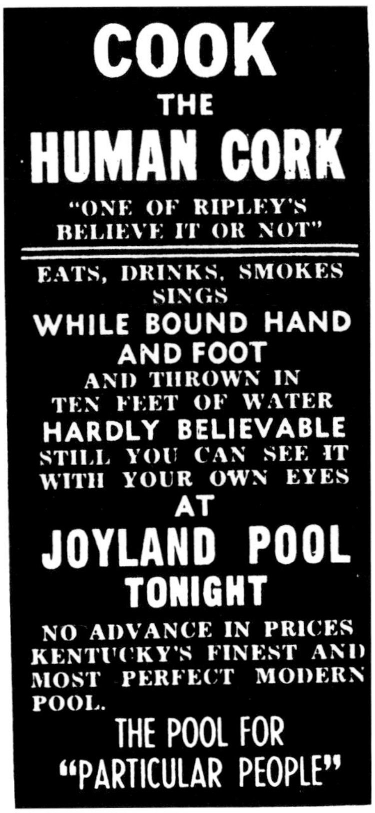

THE ONE AND ONLY HUMAN CORK, **ALAN COOKE** of BALTIMORE **could eat, drink, and sleep while floating on the water.** To prove that he couldn't (or wouldn't ?) sink, he was thrown tied, taped, and bound into Lake Michigan, numerous rivers and indoor pools, and into the Chesapeake Bay fifteen times. *Believe It or Not!* radio program guest, 1940.

THE HUMAN CORK, steel-mill worker **W. C. CAVENDER** of Pueblo, COLORADO, **relaxed for hours each day afloat while drinking soda pop,** reading a newspaper, and smoking a cigar. He enjoyed demonstrating his unusual buoyancy by allowing himself to be bound hand and foot and thrown into the pool, or as shown here, by balancing tumblers of water on his chest, forehead, and both palms. Coincidentally, Mr. Cavender **died the day the cartoon appeared. (February 11, 1953)**

Four-year-old **Billy Crawford jumped over the Cleveland Municipal Building wearing a harness attached to a balloon** that barely held him aloft! When this picture was taken, Billy had spent more than four solo hours aloft, leaping around the city. **(June 1, 1934)**

TATTOO TALENT

"Good sense is the body of poetic genius, fancy its drapery, motion its life, and imagination the soul."

SAMUEL TAYLOR COLERIDGE

"PROFESSOR" **WILLIAM LUCAS,** of St. Paul, MINNESOTA, had **his wife's name tattooed inside his mouth.** He also had stars tattooed on his earlobes, the words *Holy Ghost* tattooed on his fingers, and most of the rest of his body heavily tattooed.
(December 19, 1936)

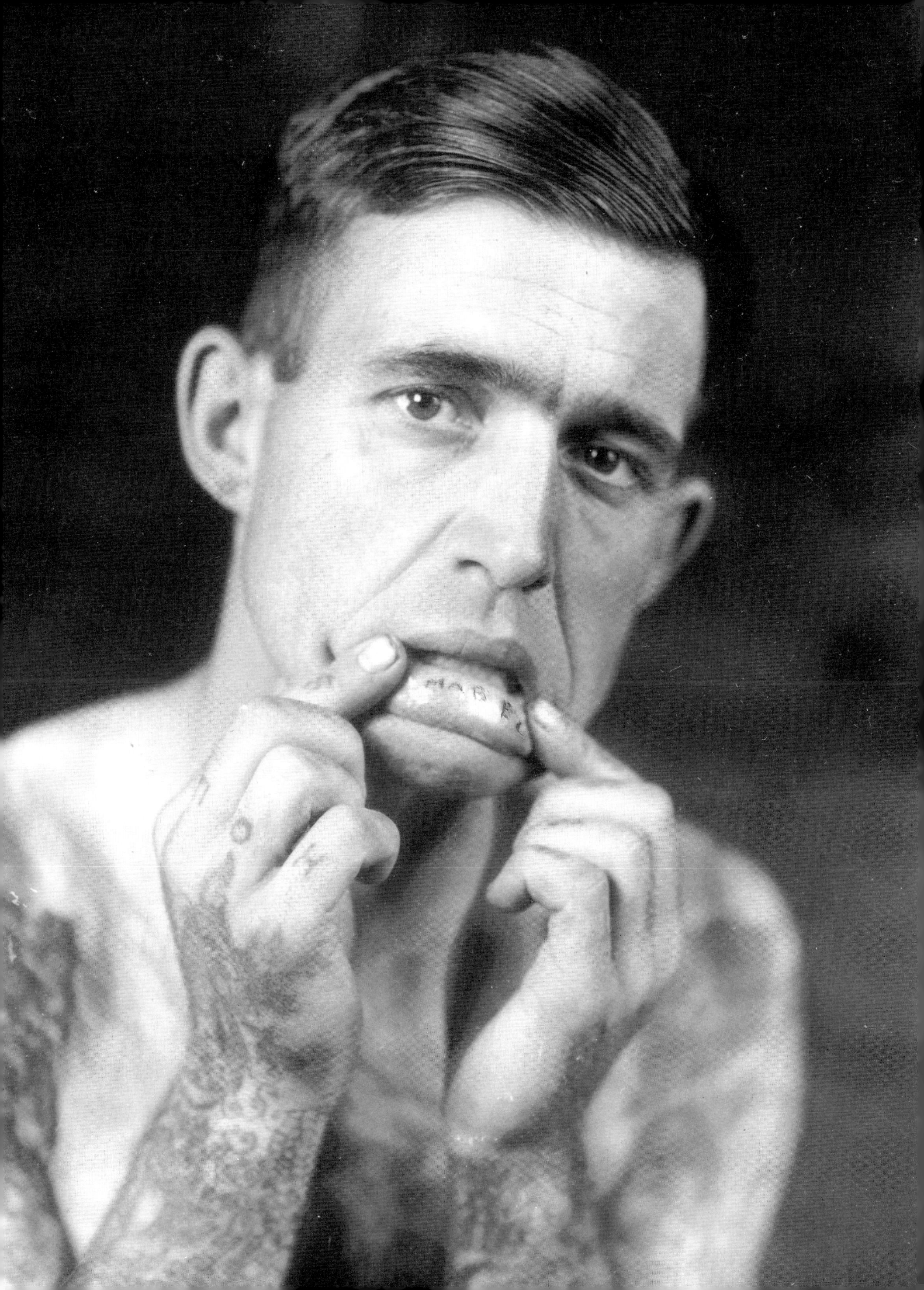

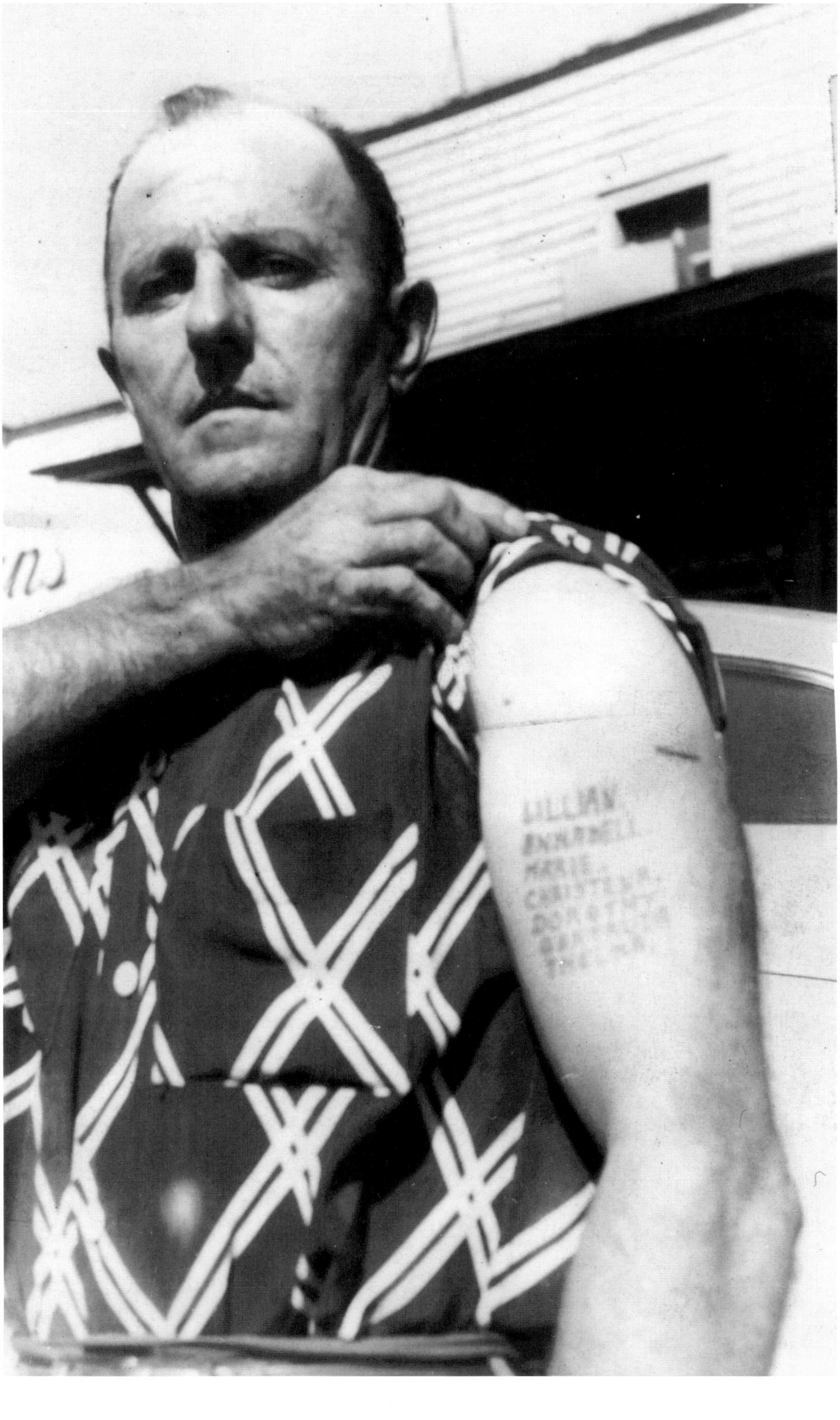

CLESTON JENKINS of Kuttawa, KENTUCKY, had **the first names of each of his seven divorced wives tattooed on his arm. (February 27, 1953)**

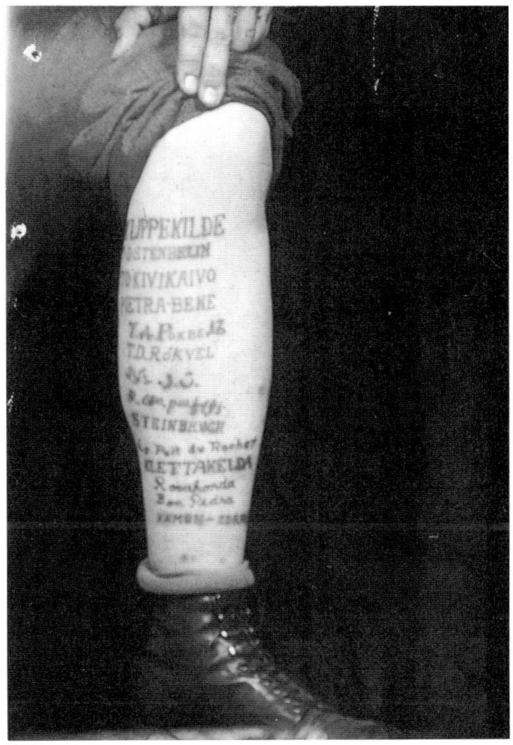

SAN FRANCISCO razor blade salesman **T. D. ROCKWELL,** THE MAN WHO COULDN'T GET LOST, **had his name and address tattooed on his body in Chinese, Japanese, English,** Hebrew, Palestinian, Greek, Danish, Swedish, Finnish, Italian, Russian, Hungarian, Arabic, Persian, Turkish, Armenian, German, French, Spanish, Portuguese, Bohemian, Polish, Gaelic, Icelandic, Morse code, Gregg shorthand, and semaphore. He originally did it, he said, **"for ease in cashing checks,"** since not only was his own address rendered on his legs but also the address of his bank! **(January 13, 1937)**

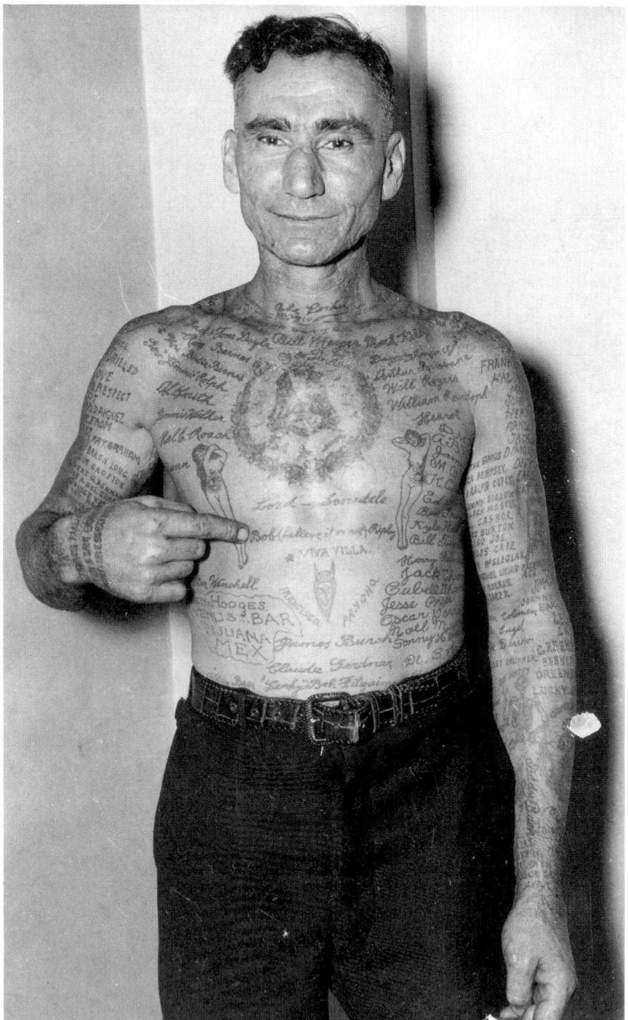

Former boxer **DICK HYLAND,** the HUMAN AUTOGRAPH ALBUM, **was tattooed from head to foot with the names of more than six hundred friends,** celebrities, and chance acquaintances. Here Hyman points at the signature of Bob (*Believe It or Not!*) Ripley, just above a dedication to Pancho Villa. Ripley's sponsor, William Randolph Hearst, was also a "signee." Hyland was a 1939 NEW YORK Odditorium performer. **(July 12, 1939)**

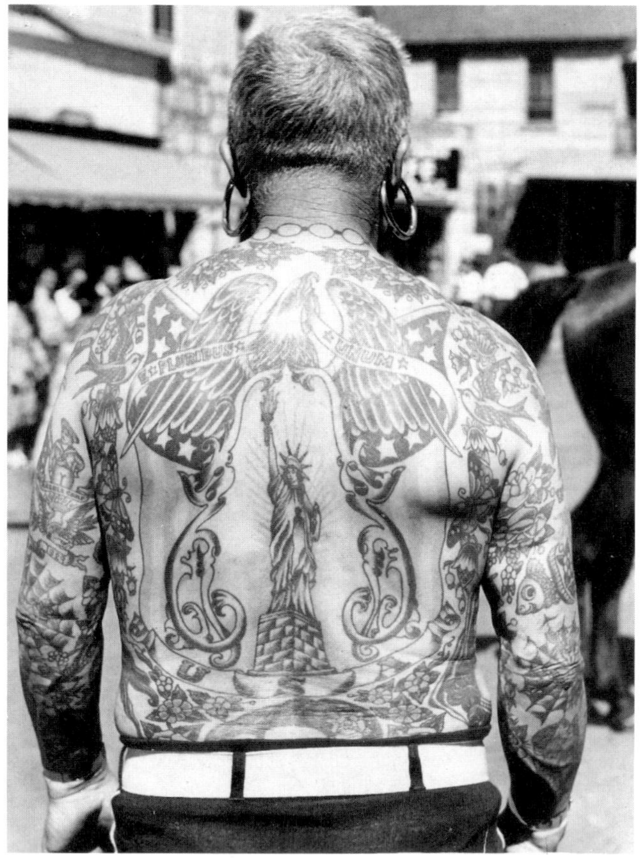

RASMUS NIELSEN (above and at right) of Angel's Camp, CALIFORNIA, **lifts a 200-pound anvil with a metal bar pierced through his nipples.** He could also lift a 115-pound rock by one nipple, and 10-pound hammers from rings through his ears. His extensive tattoos depicted giant sequoia trees and patriotic scenes, among other things. **(July 16, 1938)**

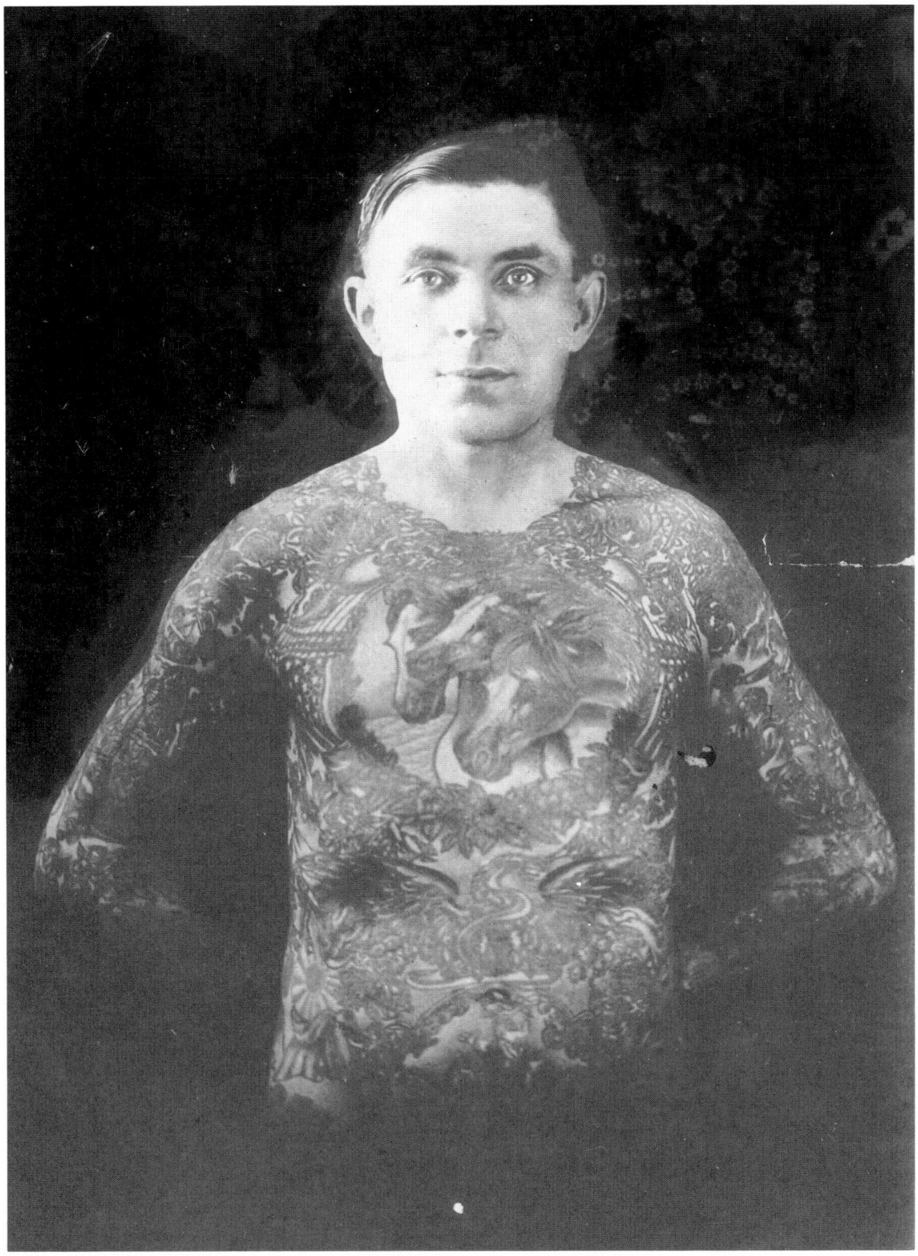

"PROFESSOR" **CHARLES WAGNER** claimed to be "one of the most artistic of tattooed people." **His back depicted a scene entitled "Child Christ and a Trip to Mars (in an airplane)."**

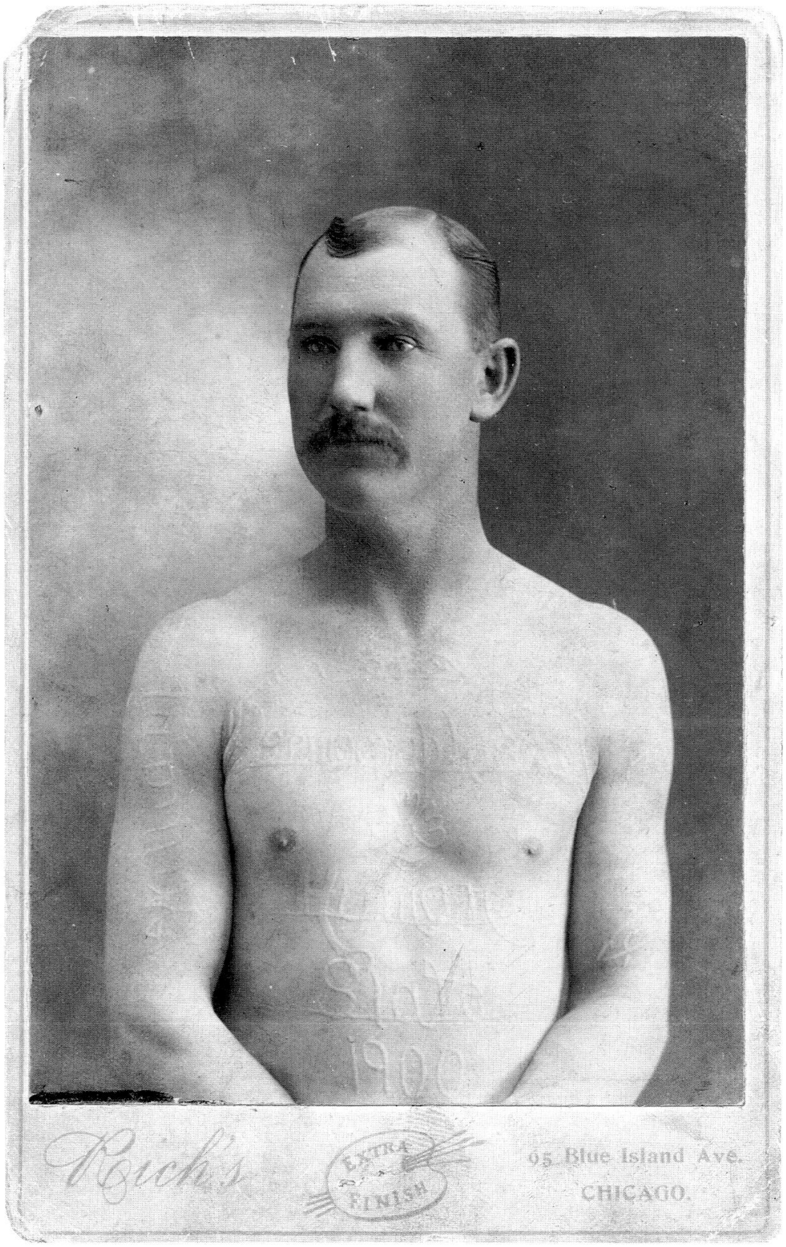

William H. Fiekling of Cambridge, Illinois, was known as the Human Slate because **his skin raised temporary welts when touched with a blunt instrument.** Apparently it all began one very hot afternoon as he was putting up hay. After each load he would jump into a cold spring to cool off. The next day he became very sick and since that time was unable to perspire except on his head and hands. Not long after that he discovered that his "lithographic skin" would swell in response to rubbing or scratching. **(November 26, 1932)**

World Champions

"He was a bold man who first swallowed an oyster."

King James I of England

Frank Antonievich won a bronze medal, a diploma, and a ten-dollar gold piece when he **cooked 100 pancakes in 22 1/2 minutes** at the Grand Central Palace in New York. He was as fancy as he was productive, tossing the flapjacks in six different pans behind him from between his legs and catching them in the same pans in front of him. **(September 10, 1945)**

MRS. W. E. UPDEGRAFF could cook sixty pies in forty-five minutes. A team of witnesses in Vinita, OKLAHOMA, reported that they each tasted excellent. **(July 10, 1933)**

World-champion chicken picker **"Buck" Fulford** of Port Arthur, Texas, **could kill, pick clean, cut up, cook, and eat a chicken in one minute and fifty seconds.** Elaborating on his technique, he explained that it took forty seconds to cut off the chicken's head and allow it to die, ten seconds for scalding, three or four seconds to pick and clean the chicken, three seconds to cut it into four portions and drop it into boiling grease, thirty seconds to cook it, followed by cooling in cracked ice, and the rest of the time was for savoring and eating the fowl. Fulford's other accomplishments included plucking and picking as many as twelve chickens in one minute. **(April 30, 1935)**

BELIEVE IT OR NOT INFORMATION BLANK

From: John Strocco
6107 B'way
Woodside L.I.

To: Believe *It* or *Not*, Inc.

BELIEVE IT OR NOT:

I can smash, with one snap of the finger as shown in above photograph, Brazil Pecans & Walnuts. In the thirty-five years that I have been doing this, I have yet to see someone else do it.

VERIFICATION: (Give names of witnesses, book reference, or other source of information, and *include photographs* if possible)

I have seen Mr. Strocco break nuts with his finger
G. L. McIntosh c/o United Shoe Machine Corp. of America. N.Y.C.
Mr. John Strocco has performed before me as described above. I. D. Mechaneck M.D. (41-25-70th St. Woodside, L.I.
Witnessed by Mr. Robert Ripley in Believe it or not office

I hereby grant to Robert Ripley and *Believe It or Not*, Inc. permission to make use of this material.

Signed John Strocco
NAME

6107 Broadway
STREET

Woodside L.I. New York
CITY

Date Jan 16, 1938

KINDLY RETURN IN STAMPED ADDRESSED ENVELOPE

Eighteen-year-old **Edd Woolf drank five gallons and thirty ounces of water,** then had a sandwich and a malt at Cheque's Confectionery in Duncan, Oklahoma. All this **in less than thirty minutes!** Woolf performed this amazing feat to win six dollars. **(November 7, 1935)**

Ed Kottwitz, four times world-champion sweet corn eater, **gnawed fifty ears of corn** at the Third Annual Ortonville (Minnesota) Sweet Corn Festival. Kottwitz was a forty-year-old South Dakota farmer. **(February 26, 1935)**

John Strocco of Woodside, Long Island, **cracked hazelnuts,** pecans, and walnuts **by smashing them with his finger. (May 4, 1938)**

LORENZO LECLET rode 3,465 miles around the circumference of the island of PUERTO RICO in three days on a borrowed bicycle, without eating or sleeping! The trip only cost a nickel: three cents for a pack of matches and two cents for a candle to light his way after dark. **(June 13, 1931)**

In an era of nonstop ballroom dancing and flagpole sitting, **ice-sitting** was a little-known avenue for competition. **Gus Simmons** (arrow) **sat for twenty-seven hours and ten minutes before being disqualified** for running a 102 degree fever (!) at this contest held at Chicago's White City Casino. **(October 17, 1933)**

ISRAEL "LUCKY SLIM" BRESSNER, BALTIMORE street cleaner, **found a penny each day for fourteen days! (March 3, 1932)**

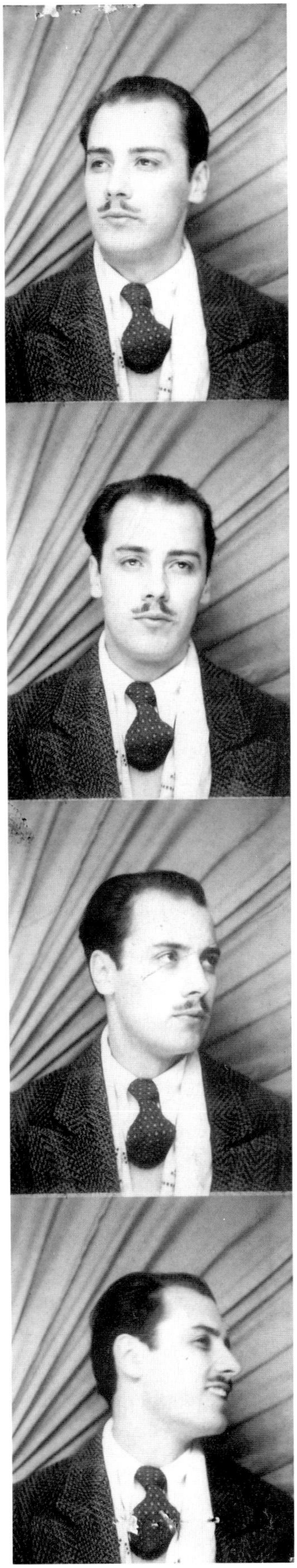

CHICAGO'S **PAULO GIGANTI** claimed to be the only **full-blooded Italian who had never eaten spaghetti** or macaroni in his life. His mother served it every day for years, but he never touched a bite. **(December 16, 1937)**

FORREST YANKEY lassoed a house-fly with a length of cotton thread in Grand Rapids, MICHIGAN. The momentous event was witnessed by his immediate family. Astoundingly, the fly lived through the unsettling experience. **(December 4, 1934)**

Hawaiian swimmer **TOMMY KAEO caught a four-pound white sea bass** off Steel Pier at Atlantic City, NEW JERSEY, with his bare hands **after swimming a quarter mile. (July 13, 1935)**

"SHARPSHOOTER SUPREME" **EDNA ALEE** of Detroit, MICHIGAN, **cut a card edgewise at a distance of sixty-three feet with her .22 caliber revolver** held as shown. She cut another card edgewise twice in succession at seventy-five feet with a .38 caliber revolver that same afternoon. **(April 13, 1938)**

Mrs. Anna E. Van Skike of Santa Monica, California, **swam over 3,000 miles *after* her sixtieth birthday.** She marked her seventieth birthday with a twenty-mile swim in the Pacific Ocean, and her seventy-second birthday by swimming around the Rainbow Pier at Long Beach singing "The Holy City" and "The Star-Spangled Banner" while holding aloft a flag in each hand. **(December 1, 1933)**

Long-distance swimmer **Fred Newton** of Clinton, Oklahoma, **swam the Mississippi River from Minneapolis to New Orleans**—a distance of approximately 2,300 miles. Newton spent a total of 742 hours in the river and claims to have gained ten pounds in the process. **His first bathing suit wore out** after 1,700 miles. He painted signs at night along the way to finance the swim. **(June 10, 1931)**

What's in a Name?

"This generation of Americans has a rendezvous with destiny."

Franklin Delano Roosevelt

SAM HELLER, a "Ham Seller" of Richmond, Virginia, shown here with the Smithfield ham he presented in person to President Coolidge. **(March 30, 1931)**

RICHMOND GROCERY CO.
INCORPORATED
RICHMOND, VIRGINIA
Hon. Calvin Coolidge
The White House
Washington, D.C.
SAM HELLER BRAND
GENUINE
SMITHFIELD HAM
DISTRIBUTED BY
RICHMOND GROCERY COMPANY
INCORPORATED
RICHMOND, VIRGINIA
NET WEIGHT
WHEN PACKED
LBS. ____ OZ.

Teller's Photograph

NAME Mr. I.Teller, Information Clerk

STREET ADDRESS Hudson Terminal Post Office

CITY AND STATE New York City

USED 3/9/35

BELIEVE IT OR NOT: I. Teller—quite an appropriate name for the information man

Rip:

BELGIAN LINE

New York, 10 PEARL ST., Tel. Bowling Green 8960-4
COMPAGNIE MARITIME BELGE S. A.
(LLOYD ROYAL)

See Blotter on Back for Sailing Dates and Steamers

NEW YORK—ANTWERP DIRECT

I. TELLER IS THE NAME OF AN INFORMATION CLERK AT THE HUDSON TERMINAL P.O. NYC.

J M Bunnell

VERIFICATION: Mr M. G. Knowles
410 Van Buren St
Bklyn Nyp.

I. TELLER was an information clerk at the Hudson Terminal Post Office in NEW YORK CITY. **(March 9, 1935)**

(Give names of witnesses, book reference, or source of information and include photographs if possible.)

KINDLY RETURN IN STAMPED ADDRESSED ENVELOPE.

Kindly notify Mr Teller when it is to be put in the newspaper Thank you Irving Teller 560 West 192 St NY City

TELEPHONE MAIN OFFICIAL

O. HOWE GOOD

RIGHT OF WAY DEPARTMENT
SOUTH BROOKLYN DIVISION
NEW YORK TELEPHONE COMPANY
205 SCHERMERHORN ST., BROOKLYN, N. Y.

Hall
ood Road
N. Y.

0104 Used 7/3/31

June 1st 1931.

Mr. Robert L.Ripley
235 East 45th St.
New York N.Y.

Dear Mr. Ripley,

Attached is the picture that you requested and you have my permission to use it for your "Believe it or not cartoons" if you need the rest of the body which is five foot five I will have to send you another.

My I add appreciation for many a good time I have had watching your features and hope that they long continue as one of the cleanest ,educational and best features on the screen.

Very Truly Yours

O. Howe Good

O.Howe Good.

P/S Strange ~~it~~ it may seem My job is a complaint agent...

O. HOWE GOOD was a complaint agent for the New York Telephone Company in BROOKLYN. **(July 3, 1931)**

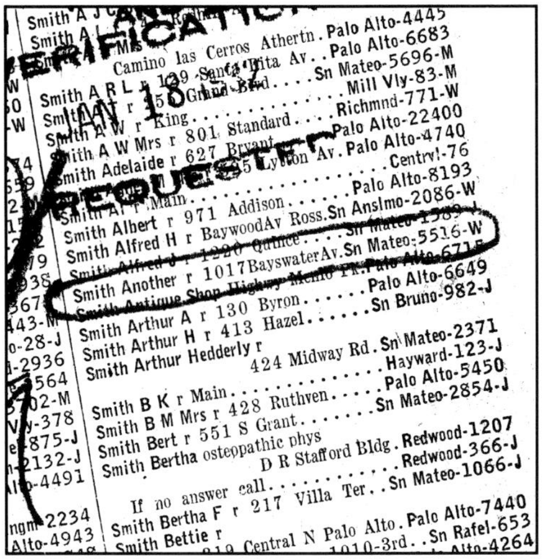

Newspaperman **ANOTHER SMITH,** who **signed his friendly letters "Just Another,"** was manager of Wide World Photos for the *New York Times.* **(August 29, 1932)**

Two radio repairmen both working at the same time at Rabeck Music Company in Olympia, WASHINGTON, **were named LES COOL and LES HOT. (July 28, 1953)**

TWO RADIO REPAIR MEN
EMPLOYED AT SAME TIME
BY RABECK MUSIC CO.
OLYMPIA, WASH.

U. S. WALKER was a mail carrier in Kansas City, MISSOURI. **(May 26, 1933)**

East met West when **MR. E. E. EAST** of West Virginia met **MR. E. E. WEST** of east Virginia at the National Business College in Roanoke, VIRGINIA. Imagine the odds! **(February 5, 1937)**

JACK FROST sold refrigerators in WASHINGTON, D.C. **(February 12, 1931)**

WASHINGTON, D.C., milkman **I. M. WISER** was married to **MAY B. WISER**. **Their child was "a little Wiser." (May 2, 1941)**

A. C. CURRENT was an electrical contractor in Tontogany, OHIO. His son's name was **D. C. CURRENT. (December 16, 1931)**

MR. PINK DUCK was a janitor in Jackson, MISSISSIPPI. **(November 27, 1933)**

MISS BIRDIE SNYDER married **MR. C. CANARY** to become **BIRDIE CANARY. (January 6, 1938)**

Native Alabaman **LEGAL TENDER FAIRCLOTH** claimed to be **the only person in the world named for currency. (October 16, 1939)**

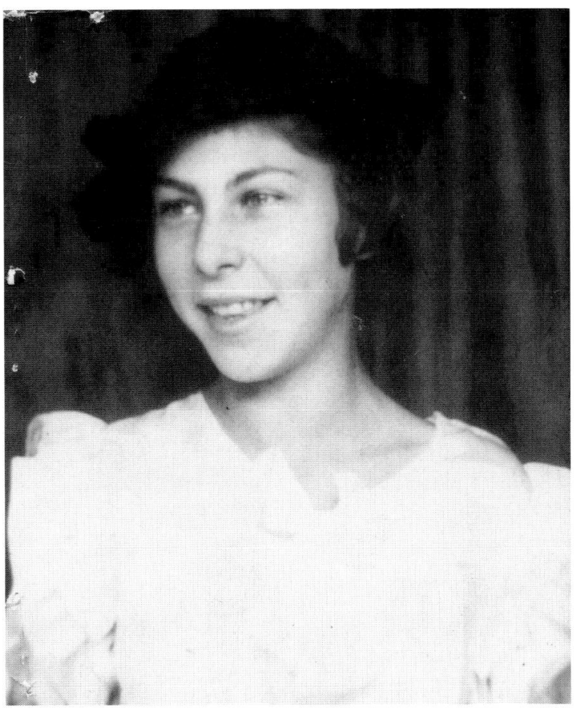

IONA FIDDLE of St. Paul, MINNESOTA, **never owned or played a fiddle. (February 23, 1935)**

WILLIAM WILLIAMS lived on **Williams Street in Williamsburg,** KANSAS. **(May 13, 1936)**

ATTA ATTA, an immigrant **from Ata, in Attica,** GREECE. **(March 21, 1940)**

VIRGINIA HIGHT was the librarian for the **Virginia Heights** School in ROANOKE. **(September 20, 1941)**

An eye specialist in Hillsboro, OHIO, was named **C. SITES. (February 28, 1935)**

H. M. BALMER was a **funeral director** in Fort Collins, Colorado. **(November 8, 1934)**

NINA CLOCK passed her time in St. Paul, Minnesota. **(June 3, 1931)**

THE CLIPPER BROTHERS were barbers in Bakersfield, California. **(November 9, 1951)**

GEORGE KOPMAN was a police officer in San Francisco for more than thirty years. **(April 22, 1935)**

MR. AB C DEFGHI lived in Villa Park, Illinois, **with his alphabetic name. (May 28, 1935)**

MISS ANNIE RAINER SHINE grew banana plants in Luverne, Alabama. **(March 3, 1933)**

HANNAH LABAL married **BOB OTTO** on November (the eleventh month) 22, and lived at 1991 33rd Drive in the Bronx. **All the names and numbers associated with their wedding and address could be read backwards and forwards. (October 30, 1947)**

MR. SANTA C. KLAUS paid $225.50 cash to the Tennessee Electric Power Company for a DeLuxe 837 Frigidaire in Chattanooga, Tennessee, **seventeen days before Christmas. (December 21, 1944)**

MR. A. BALL PITCHER of Melrose Park, Illinois, **never threw a ball** in the seventy years of his life. **(September 23, 1933)**

MISS HELEN FERNAL was a peace-loving girl from Portland, Oregon. **(May 21, 1930)**

MISS MERRY CHRISTMAS DAY was born on December 25, 1903, in Bellingham, WASHINGTON. In submitting her daughter's name and picture to Ripley, Merry's mother asked it not appear "alongside a three-legged calf or some other monstrosity." **(December 25, 1932)**

When her name appeared in the Ripley's cartoon, **DINA MIGHT was just a young girl** from Flint, MICHIGAN. **(September 22, 1932)**

CALIFORNIA POPPE lived in Inglewood, **CALIFORNIA. (July 8, 1933)**

MISS CALI FORNIA lived in San Pedro, **CALIFORNIA. (October 28, 1931)**

MRS. ALMA MATER was a housewife in Tulsa, OKLAHOMA. **(January 31, 1933)**

DOCTOR LAWYER was mayor of Ironwood, MICHIGAN. **(August 6, 1947)**

ICCOLO MICCOLO played a piccolo for the LOS ANGELES Philharmonic Orchestra. **(July 26, 1935)**

DEEP C. FISHER hated fishing because he didn't like to hurt animals of any kind. Instead, he sold real estate in SAN FRANCISCO. **(February 7, 1939)**

MISS NELLIE MAY FLY married an aviator who worked for Richfield Oil in Fresno, CALIFORNIA. **(February 4, 1936)**

TWINKLE STARR came to Ripley's attention when she was struck by a car in Portland, OREGON. She recovered from her injuries. **(June 26, 1931)**

B. A. CRANK may have turned things around on his farm in Waldo, ARKANSAS, but was reported in the local paper to have **"plenty of mental calibre" nonetheless. (December 27, 1932)**

In Charleston, WEST VIRGINIA, **an automobile frame and axle repair shop was run by FRANK FRAME and JOE AXLE. (March 30, 1943)**

PARSON B. R. PARSONS lived in the **parsonage** on **Parsons Street** in Saranac, MICHIGAN. **(October 13, 1935)**

A. FISH was in charge of fish distribution in OREGON. **(November 20, 1932)**

The school dentist for the Burlington, IOWA, Independent School District was **DR. H. A. TOOTHACRE. (November 30, 1932)**

BARBER SAUL of NEW YORK was **the seventh son of a seventh son,** and he and every other male in his family for the previous three generations were barbers. **(March 2, 1942)**

JOHN PAINTER was a painter and paperhanger in Centralia, ILLINOIS. **(February 17, 1955)**

Novel Ideas

"Imagination is more important than knowledge."

Albert Einstein

Shown here is **the biggest broom ever made. It was thirteen feet across the base and forty feet tall.** Made in Deshler, NEBRASKA, at the Deshler Broom Factory (at the time the largest broom factory in the world), the giant broom was made to celebrate the fiftieth anniversary of the factory. Standing in front are the town mayor and the president of the factory. Later the broom was dismantled and recycled to make 1,440 standard-sized brooms. **(November 14, 1940)**

GOLDEN 1940
SITTLER
DRUG
CO.
RITZ
DRUG STORE
Coca-Cola
DRUGS
PRESCRIPTIONS

The World's Largest Strawberry Shortcake was a nineteen-year tradition at the time of this photograph in 1954. Lebanon, OREGON, was the site of this whopping dessert, which, with toppings, weighed in at over 5,000 pounds and **served a modest 12,000 persons. (September 21, 1954)**

QUEEN OF THE CLAM FESTIVAL AND HER COURT ON HER THRONE in **the World's Largest Frying Pan** in Long Beach, WASHINGTON, in 1941. **(December 2, 1948)**

Here CHICAGO auto mechanic **JOSEPH STEINLAUF** is shown posed with two of his bicycle inventions: **a bedroom bicycle and a sewing machine bike.** Steinlauf's ingenious bikes, including one built with guns (in firing condition), appeared in the Ripley's cartoon feature a number of times. The gun bike weighed 350 pounds and carried fifteen different antique guns ranging from a 1780 Chinese flintlock to a Springfield repeating rifle used in the Indian Wars. **(April 30, 1939)** (bedroom bike) and **(October 23, 1939)** (sewing machine bike)

Former farmer **Roy Gardner** of Mason City, Illinois, was a star attraction at Ripley's Chicago Odditorium in 1934. He had **eighty pipes and strings** in his set and claimed to have spent three hours per day just tuning up. Both hands, both feet, and even his head got in on the act while **he played all of these instruments simultaneously.**

Although blind, **Anton Pagani could simultaneously whistle and play the accordion and the cello,** frequently entertaining crowds at theaters and Shrine Temples within range of his home in LaSalle, Illinois. **(April 29, 1940)**

In Bristol, VERMONT, a farmer named **HOWARD HASELTINE had a set of musical wood** on which he could play tunes with a hammer. Over the years he tuned them by sawing or splitting off pieces to raise the pitch until they were perfectly tuned. **(May 27, 1935)**

After ten years' practice, **ARTHUR SCHULTZ** of Hamtramck, MICHIGAN, taught himself to **play the song "Black Eyes" on the piano with both his hands upside down. (March 29, 1939)**

Evangelist **CLYDE VAN PATTEN** attracted crowds to hear his sermons by promising to **perform musical numbers with his nose.** Based in Highland Park, MICHIGAN, Van Patten attended revival meetings throughout the upper Midwest. **(March 16, 1934)**

MRS. WILLIS N. WARD and **MRS. JOHN HOPPEMATH,** regular winter tourists visiting in Mount Dora, FLORIDA, often sported "Eskimo-style" **clothing made from *Florida Times Union* newspapers.** They saved winter issues of the paper for seven years to make the costumes, each of which required 700 yards of thread to assemble. **(August 17, 1936)**

JOSEPHINE-JOSEPH, born half-man, half-woman. He/she had a traveling show called the Josephine-Joseph show, which featured a number of unusual people. **Circa 1930s.**

JOHN PECINOVSKY, Lime Springs, IOWA'S **HALF-AND-HALF MAN,** was **of Bohemian descent** and ran a tavern in Bonair, four miles northwest of Cresco, in Howard County. He dressed in **different colors** on both sides and cut his hair and **shaved differently** on each side. **(May 22, 1940)**

Six hundred Colorado sales tax tokens—with a combined value of $1.20—went into making the ski costume **AUDREY TWITCHELL** wore when she showed up to schuss down the Broadmoor–Glen Cove ski course on Pike's Peak. **(July 4, 1938)**

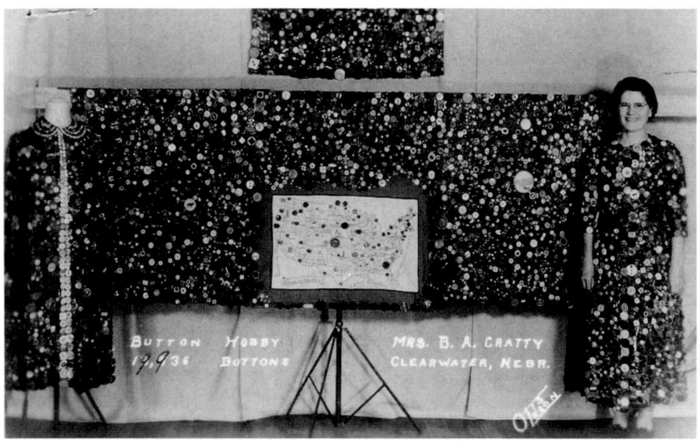

MRS. B. A. CRATLY of Clearwater, NEBRASKA, for many years collected buttons, but only if she could get them without paying for them. Through trading and exchanging, she had **gathered 19,922 different kinds of buttons from thirty-seven different countries** at the time this picture was taken. **(December 12, 1945)**

Bachelor **OWEN TOTTEN** of Mt. Erie, ILLINOIS, wore a button suit he **covered with 5,600 buttons, "no two alike." (March 31, 1946)**

Mission, TEXAS, the self-proclaimed "Home of the Grapefruit," was also home to **WILMA BETH SHULKE,** who decorated this **dress with cross-sections of corn cobs trimmed with orange peels. (May 23, 1940)**

Not to be outdone by her rivals elsewhere in Texas, **VIRGINIA WINN** of Mercedes, TEXAS, modeled a **forty-pound evening dress covered with nearly 60,000 grains of corn** stitched to the material one at a time. **(February 11, 1940)**

In order to push new uses for turkey products, the Chamber of Commerce of Cuero, TEXAS, in 1947 sponsored a fashion show for turkey feather attire. **BEVERLY BELL** spent five hours making this entry, which included **shoes made from the quill ends of the feathers. (August 4, 1947)**

In 1933, **William T. Washington "hand tailored" an 850-pound ball of string during lunch hours** while at the Conservation Department at a Detroit post office. The ball was six feet in diameter. In a letter dated March 13, 1940, Ripley tried unsuccessfully to obtain the string ball for the Odditorium in New York City.

A recluse named **S. S. STAMBAUGH** for several years collected **eight-inch lengths of string** from a local flour mill in Tulare, CALIFORNIA, and by knotting and winding the pieces was able to build a three-foot-diameter twine ball in less than two years. Upon seeing the huge creation a friendly visitor calculated that **Stambaugh had tied 463,040 knots in nearly 132 miles of twine to make the 320-pound ball. (March 22, 1938)**

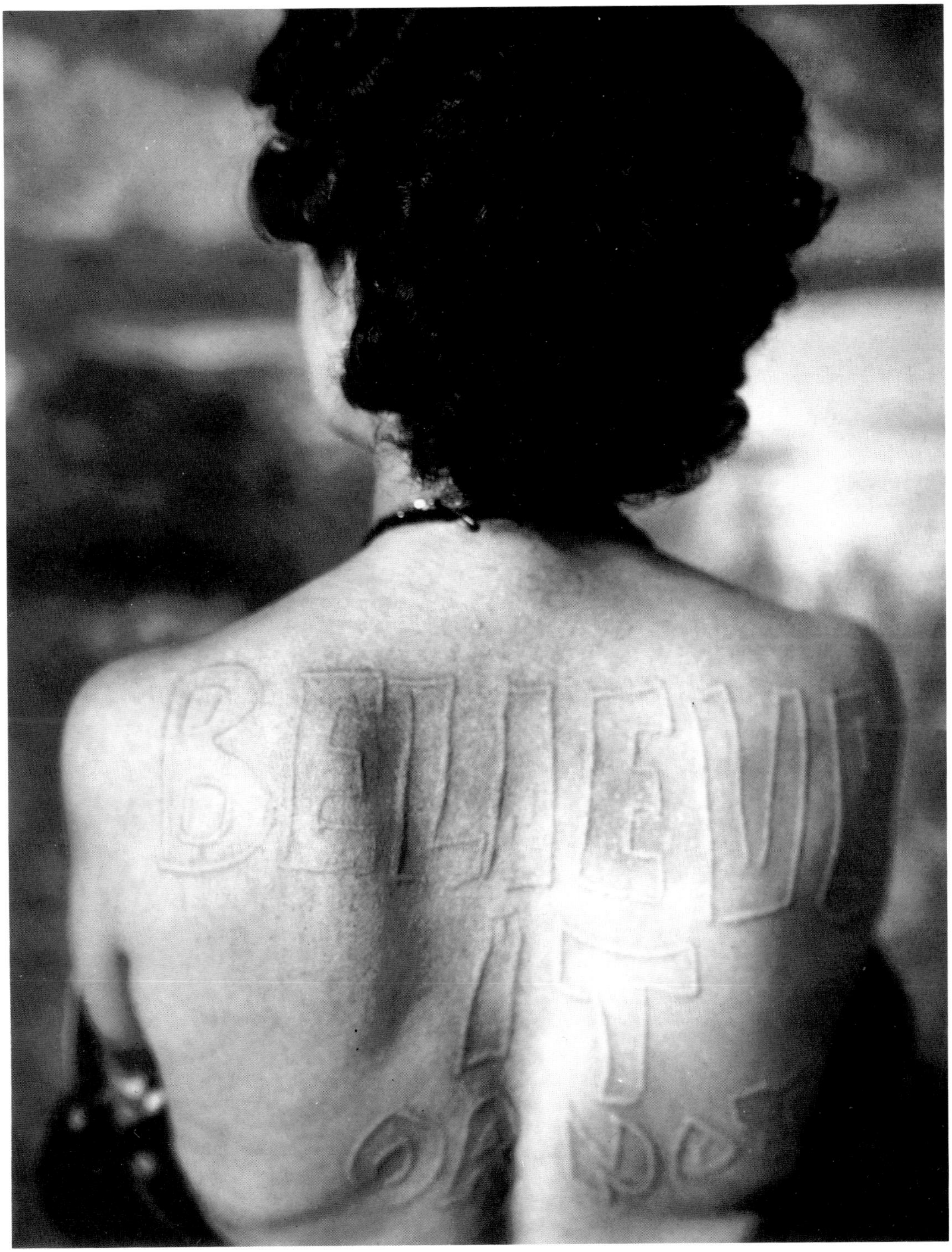

Rosa Barthelme—The Human Slate.

Museums

Ripley's Believe It or Not! Museum
4960 Clifton Hill
Niagara Falls, Ontario L2G 3N4
Canada
(416) 356-2238

Ripley's Believe It or Not! Museum
Cranberry Village
Cavendish, P.E.I. C0A 1N0
Canada
(902) 963-3444

Ripley's Believe It or Not! Museum
7850 Beach Boulevard
Buena Park, California 90620
(714) 522-1155

Ripley's Believe It or Not! Museum
175 Jefferson Street
San Francisco, California 94133
(415) 771-6188

Ripley's Believe It or Not! Museum
19 San Marco Avenue
St. Augustine, Florida 32084
(904) 824-1606

Ripley's Believe It or Not! Museum
250 S.W. Bay Boulevard
Mariner Square
Newport, Oregon 97365
(503) 265-2206

Ripley's Believe It or Not! Museum
901 North Ocean Boulevard
Myrtle Beach, South Carolina 29578
(803) 448-2331

Ripley's Believe It or Not! Museum
800 Parkway
Gatlinburg, Tennessee 37738
(615) 436-5096

Ripley's Believe It or Not! Museum
301 Alamo Plaza (across from the Alamo)
San Antonio, Texas 78205
(512) 224-9299

Ripley's Believe It or Not! Museum
601 East Safari Parkway
Grand Prairie, Texas 75050
(214) 263-2391

Ripley's Believe It or Not! Museum
115 Broadway
Wisconsin Dells, Wisconsin 53965
(608) 254-2184

Ripley's Believe It or Not! Museum
P.O. Box B1
Raptis Plaza, Cavill Mall
Surfer's Paradise, Queensland 4217
Australia
(61) 7-592-0040

Ripley's Believe It or Not! Museum
Units 5 and 6
Ocean Boulevard
South Promenade
Blackpool, Lancashire
England FY4 IEZ
(44) 253-41033 x 286

Ripley's Believe It or Not! Museum
6780 Hollywood Boulevard
Los Angeles, California 90028
(213) 466-6335

Ripley's Believe It or Not! Museum
Radhuspladsen 57
DK-1550 Copenhagen V
Denmark
(45) 33-918991

Ripley's Believe It or Not! Museum
8201 International Drive
Orlando, Florida 32819
(407) 872-3081

Ripley's Believe It or Not! Museum
Aunque Ud. No Lo Crea de Ripley
Londres No. 4
Col. Juarez
C.P. 06600
Mexico, D.F.
(52) 5546 7670

Ripley's Believe It or Not! Museum
Ripley's Museo DeAunque Usted No Lo Crea
Morales #215, Centro Historico
C.P. 44100
Guadalajara, Jal. Mexico
(523) 614-8487

Ripley's Believe It or Not! Museum
The Peak Tower, Level 3
The Peak, Hong Kong
(852) 2849-0818

Ripley's Believe It or Not! Museum
Royal Garden Plaza
218 Moo 10, Beach Road
Nongprue, Banglamung
Chonburi 20260 Pattaya, Thailand
(66) 38-710-294

Ripley's Believe It or Not! Museum
1441 Boardwalk
Atlantic City, New Jersey 08401
(609) 347-2001

Ripley's Believe It or Not! Museum
3326 W. Highway 76
Branson, Missouri 65616
(417) 337-5300

Ripley's Believe It or Not! Museum
140 N. Cache Street, P.O. Box 954
Jackson Hole, Wyoming 83001
(307) 734-0000

Ripley's Believe It or Not! Museum
Pier Building, 401 Atlantic Avenue
Ocean City, Maryland 21842
(410) 289-5600

www.ripleys.com

Cecil E. King

USED 11/3/41

Los Angeles, California
Aug. 25, 1941

Mr. Robert Ripley
c/o King Feature Syndicate.

Dear Mr. Ripley,

A few days ago I read in the Los Angeles Examiner, your cartoon which featured a woman in Chicago who can read a book upside down. I have alway been able to do so, as fast and accurate as when book is right side up. I did not think it was an accomplishment to rate sending the fact in to you, altho' my friends have urged me to do so, many times. However, I will be very pleased if you could use this fact; and I'd be very glad to send you a picture, and anyway to prove my statement. I am an amateur poet, having had over one hundred poems published in various newspapers thro' out the United States.

Very Sincerely Yours,
(Miss) Cecil Edna King.
240 W. Santa Barbara Ave.
Los Angeles, Calif.

PAGE 98

Siegmund Klein
PHYSICAL CULTURE STUDIO

USED 11/8/41

717 SEVENTH AVENUE
(AT 48TH STREET)
NEW YORK CITY

Aug.25,1941

Mr. Robert L.Ripley
235 East 45 St.,
New York City

My Dear Mr. Ripley:

It has been a long time since I have mailed you something about myself for publication in your "Believe It Or Not".

I have in the past few weeks made a few experiments in hand-Balancing and think that the enclosed picture with the explanatory remarks on the back explain what I have done.

In the event that you use this in your column, I do not know if it would be advisable to let readers know how I timed this or not. I had to find out about the rest periods and how long it takes to do the "dips" through experiment.

Much to my surprise I found that the sets of "five" for 10 times went the easiest, and that "3" dips of 17 sets about the hardest, but think that the 5 sets of 10 "dips", would be the best one to use if you think it worthy of your column.

I also have a picture showing the full hand stand, but thought that the position of the chest touching the bench each time would be more appropiate.

There are many thousands of "hand-balacers" in the country that I know would like to try this, as I hold quite a few records on this type of balancing.

Trusting to hewr from you at your earliest conveniece, and I would appreciate hearing from you if you will use this, the approximate date.

Yours sincerely,
Siegmund Klein

The Studio, Located In The Heart of New York's Theatrical District, Is The Only Gymnasium Of Its Kind In The World

PAGE 143

IVanhoe 1395

Larry Foto Service
PRESS - COMMERCIAL - AERIAL PHOTOGRAPHY
8097 DWYER
DETROIT - MICHIGAN

USED 2/2/42

November 31, 1941

Mr. Robert Ripley
% King Features Syndicate Inc.
235 E. 45th. Street
N.Y. N.Y.

Dear Mr Ripley:

Enclosed is 1-8x10 glossy photograph of Bill Wausmann carrying a pencil under his ear, instead of on his ear. Mr. Wausmann works at the Mt. Elliot Recreation in Detroit.

I am Submitting this photograph for publication at your usual rates.

3rd. class return postage is enclosed should the photograph be unacceptable.

Memo to send both sent to B. McD at Mam. on 1/23/42

Sincerely yours,
L. Jamrisko Jr.
L. Jamrisko Jr.

W. ROSS McCAIN, PRESIDENT
AETNA
W. N. ACHENBACH, MANAGER
WESTERN DEPARTMENT
410 N. MICHIGAN AVE., CHICAGO, ILL.

BUTTON SUIT — OVER 5600 BUTTONS — NO TWO ALIKE

USED 3/31/46

S. R. YOHE - Insurance

Mt. Erie, Illinois
Dec 14th 1945

Post Dispatch
St Louis Mo Dear Sir:

Enclosed find Picture of Mr Owen Totton of Mt Erie Ill a Bachlor Dress in his full Suit and Hat Covered With Some Over 5600 Button No Two alike Please Insurt in your Believe It or Not Ripley Collum

And Oblige
S R Yohe

PAGE 198